Captain
Reifer

Captain Reifer

The Battle for What Was Already Lost

Alex Iser Reifer

LIBRARY *of the* HOLOCAUST

Washington, D.C.

ISBN: 978-1-882326-11-2
Library of Congress Control Number: 2012938726

Library of the Holocaust Foundation
PO Box 1651
Silver Spring, Maryland 20915
800-651-9350
www.LibraryoftheHolocaust.org

Manufactured in the United States of America

Contents

Acknowledgments

I wish to thank my cousin, Mary Reifer Weissman, for all her help. Without her excellent eye in correcting my mistakes and her editorial assistance in putting my manuscript into shape, I would not have been able to finish.

My daughter, Annemarie Reifer, volunteered her time and effort to turn my handwritten story into a typed manuscript. I am very grateful for her assistance.

My wife, Susana, read over this many times and made invaluable contributions.

The guidance that my son, Brian Reifer, has lent towards the publication of this book should also be acknowledged.

Lastly, I wish to thank Jeremy Kay from the Library of the Holocaust Foundation for agreeing to put my book into published form and help make it as readable and accessible as possible for future generations.

One
Childhood

I was born February 7, 1921 in the city of Oswiecim, Poland. I was the first born, and a party was given for me when I was circumcised at 8 days old. I lived in one of my grandfather's apartments, on Koszcielina street #16, with my father, my mother and a maid. Since in 1921 there was no running water in the apartment, the maid would go out to the water station, several hundred feet away, and bring water to the apartment. She would carry the water on specially crafted wooden carriers attached to her shoulders, so as not to make many trips. She would bring the water into the kitchen, where it was stored in a barrel in a corner, next to the cabinet where the dishes were stored. There was a bucket next to the barrel of water and a towel to wash oneself; this was the way we kept clean. There was a large stove in the kitchen to burn coal or wood.

At the early age of two and a half, my parents enrolled me in a private Jewish school. I was picked up in the morning and dropped off after school. My mother would give me two slices of bread with margarine and an apple for lunch. At six o'clock, we all sat down and had dinner together, praying before and after every meal. A typical dinner consisted of chicken soup with Matzo balls, boiled beef with mashed potatoes and baked plums for dessert.

I seemed to have an excellent teacher in school, because at the age of three, I was already reading from the Jewish prayer books.

I remember walking to the synagogue with my father for Sabbath every Friday evening and every Saturday morning. Several times a month, I was invited to my grandparents' home for dinner, which my grandmother prepared and it was excellent. Sitting with my grandfather after dinner, he would ask me what I had learned in school the previous week. I would tell him of my studies and read from the Jewish prayer book (Siddur). Even though I was very good, my grandfather still corrected me often. Then my grandmother would offer me a slice of apple strudel and some orange which I quickly devoured. I would thank my grandparents, give them each a kiss and head back to my parents' home.

Soon my mother became pregnant and gave birth to my brother Leopold, or Lipu for short. My brother also had a Bris (circumcision) and a party. The maid was now taking care of Lipu, as she had done for me. Soon Lipu would be old enough to laugh and play. My brother and I got along very well, and we would spend the afternoons together after I would return home from school.

My teacher, Rabbi Leiser Foniu was a very wise man. By the age of four, I was speaking Polish, German and

Yiddish. I began learning Hebrew and preparing for a "Chemesh" party when I turned five. The party took place on a Saturday. The next day, Sunday, I started in a new school, with Rabbi Shamu Scherer. This more advanced school is where I would study Talmud.

I remember playing with my friends, Salomon Better, Shmolek Broner, Shmilel Lichter and Jankel Tadanier. We would discuss our studies, playing in the park called Platen until it began to get dark, when we would return home. Salomon Better, who is my friend to this day, lived in Straubing, Germany after having been liberated, and now resides in Israel.

As I continued to study the Talmud in school and with my grandfather, my mother gave birth to son number three. This brother was named Manele, who also had a Bris and a party.

I continued to go to the synagogue with my father and grandfather and began to pray what is called Mincha and Mariv.

My mother would tuck me in every night and tell me about her parents who lived in Tarnow, a nearby city. My mother was very kind and caring and always made each one of her sons feel special.

I recall one special Shabbat when I was asked to say the "brachas" (prayers) over the wine. I did an excellent job and my father and grandfather were proud of me. My mother served a special meal consisting of carp, gefillte fish, chicken soup with noodles, rice and vegetables. We also had brisket of beef, carrots, salad and of course, her famous apple strudel for dessert with tea.

When I was six years old, my maternal grandparents came to visit. My grandfather Hirsch Joseph, a sofer, or scroll writer, for Torah in the city of Tarnow, was an extremely educated man.

My father owned a grocery store and my mother helped him every day. Every Thursday I would go with my mother to the market to buy items for the store and for our home, such as potatoes, beans and chickens, which would then have to be killed in the Jewish tradition by a man called a Shoched. He would slit the throat of the chicken, so that it would not feel any pain. He charged twenty-five groshen (twenty-five cents). At twelve years old, I started helping my father in the store, packing flour by the kilo, potatoes, cigarettes and other assorted items.

From the age of six, I would go to the Mikveh (ritual bath) with my father every Friday morning. We brought soap and towels. This Mikveh was a building with several floors. The dressing rooms were on the second floor and the bathtubs were on the main floor. There were about 50 large bathtubs in an open room without any separations. The Mikveh itself was in the basement. For me it was like a Jacuzzi, and I felt truly privileged to take a dip there. The bathing took about an hour. My father and I would then usually visit my uncle Joseph Lauber and his wife Rivke, my father's older sister. They had a wholesale leather goods store and were suppliers to large shoe manufacturers. After each visit, my aunt would always give me two groshen (two cents), along with a kiss. Their daughter Esther (Ecia) and I became very close.

My mother gave birth to my third brother, Chaim. Once again, we had a Bris and a party for him.

In Oswiecim, we boys, including my best friend, Salomon Better, would meet every Saturday after dinner. We stayed out until it was time to return home for Havdalah services, where we would wish each other a good week (Shaledshideh). We often had conversations with our fathers and learned about business.

When I was six and a half, my grandparents invited me to travel with them to the city of Krinica for vacation, and I was very excited. My grandparents ordered two horses and a buggy to take us to the railroad station. It took many hours by train, but when we arrived it took only 10 minutes to the hotel. This was a kosher hotel, with two rooms reserved with a bathroom. We unpacked, had lunch, prayed and relaxed. The following day after breakfast, we went into the hills and drank a special water called Krinichanka. Then we returned to the hotel to eat, relax and sleep. I remember the weather was great and the air pure and clean. The time I spent in Krinica was wonderful. I couldn't wait to tell my parents all about it.

At seven, my parents enrolled me in the Polish school. My mother accompanied me the first day and bought my books. When we returned home that day, the first thing she did was take me across the street and introduce me to a tutor to help me in the Polish school.

From then on, every morning I would wake up at six, wash and pray, eat breakfast and go to Polish school, which started at eight a.m. and ended at noon. First we learned our ABCs and I was very proud when the teacher tested me, because I had already been taught to read. At two p.m., I would begin Hebrew school, which lasted for four hours. After school, at six p.m., I would go home to meet my father and grandfather to go to the synagogue to pray.

My grandfather's eyesight became very poor (he had cataracts) and the doctors told him he needed an operation. My grandfather called my father's younger brother, Iser, who lived in Vienna, Austria and was in the banking business. Uncle Iser told my grandfather to have his operation in Czechoslovakia and my grandfather agreed. Several weeks later, my grandparents travelled to Prague to see the doctors there. They set a date for the operation and at the doctor's suggestion, operated first on one eye, and scheduled the other eye for later. Upon returning to our city, my grandfather visited his regular doctor. The vision in the eye which had been operated on was completely gone. He was practically blind. I would take him to his doctor's appointments and afterwards ask him how he felt.

"Not so good," he would say. He told me he didn't think he would ever be able to see again. I began to cry and asked my grandfather not to worry, that I would be his eyes.

My daily routine changed from that day on. Every morning I would first go to my grandfather's home help him.

A few years later, my grandfather told me that I was named after his father. He seemed very proud of that.

When I was nine, my mother gave birth to my fourth

brother, Hersch Josef, and, of course, he too had a Bris and a party in his honor.

It was only a few weeks later that my father registered me at another Jewish school with Rabbi Wileford, who taught Talmud. My schedule quickly became hectic: I would wake up at six in the morning to go to my grandfather's house to be his eyes, then head to the Polish school at eight until one p.m. when I'd go to the Jewish school which lasted until five. After the Jewish school, I'd go to the tutor across the street to prepare for the Polish school the next day. At six p.m., I would take my grandfather to the synagogue to pray, then bring him home before continuing to my house. Saturday, Shabbos, the routine would change. I'd wake up at seven and get my grandfather ready for synagogue in a black silk overcoat and a mink hat called a Shtramel. After the service, we would go home and eat, and sing songs called Zmires, which are Shabbat songs. When the meal was over, I was able to go out and play with my friends.

At the age of 10, my mother registered me in the 4th grade in the Polish school. It was there that I met a new friend whose parents had a farm with cows and horses. He invited me there, but I needed my mother's permission. The next day, my mother waited for me outside school, so that I could introduce her to my friend and his mother. After we all got acquainted, we went to the farm, which took about 30 minutes.

My friend told his mother that I going to come back for some fresh milk. The next day, I walked to the farm with a cup. My friend's mother was in the barn milking the cow, and took my cup and filled it. That was the first time I had seen someone milk a cow and when I tasted the milk, I realized that it was warm and very tasty. From then on, I walked to the farm every evening and drank two cups of fresh milk. The only nights I did not go were Friday, Saturday and Sunday.

That was the time in the Jewish school when Rabbi Wileford taught us the meaning of respect; that we should have respect for everybody, especially our parents, grandparents and teachers. Rabbi Wileford used to say that when somebody gave you something, you must always say thank you.

Two

The Bobover Rebbe

L ater that year, my father registered me in a school for advanced learning, known as the Bobover Yeshiva. Even for we younger chidren, it was practically like a university of Jewish learning. The rabbi was a member of my own family, Rabbi David Reifer.

I was encouraged to be very religious and grew the side curls, called *payes*. Rabbi David Reifer was an excellent teacher and seemed to know the Talmud in its entirety. He would explain Gemara and how generations of Rabbis and teachers interpreted the books of the Torah. It was also his task to prepare me for my Bar Mitzvah which would take place when I turned 13.

Rabbi Reifer organized at trip to Tchebinia to visit the head of the Bobover Chasidim, the Bobover Rebbe himself. My grandfather offered to pay for all the expenses of the trip if my parents would allow it. I ran home to ask my parents for their permission and they agreed. A week later, the rabbi gathered 10 kids from the school, rented a wagon with 2 horses and a driver, and we set off to

Tchebinia. My brother Lipu would take my grandfather to the synagogue while I was away.

It took many hours by wagon to reach Tchebinia, but we finally arrived. The next day was Shabbos, and we dressed in our best clothes and went to the synagogue. When the Bobover Rebbe entered, everybody stood up. The cantor began praying and everybody joined in. As I looked around, I noticed that everybody had his own siddur. After the service, we all turned to our neighbor to say "Gut Shabbos," a good Sabbath! I made my way up to the Bobover Rebbe to touch him and was very happy when I did. His name was Ben Zion Halberstam.

When we returned to the place where we were staying, we prayed before the meal a magnificent dinner consisting of gefillte fish, chicken soup, boiled chicken with vegetables, and apple compote for dessert. The next day, we again went to the synagogue to pray, eat challah and honey cake, and drink tea. We then toured the city and did not return to the synagogue until the evening for Havdalah service, after which we had dinner and retired to our rooms. The next morning, we packed our belongings and returned home. My parents and brothers were very interested in my trip, of course, and wouldn't stop asking me for all the details. I then went immediately to see my grandfather to thank him for paying for my trip. He too wanted to know all of the details. He told me that if I wanted to go back in a few months to visit the Bobover Rebbe, he would again pay for my trip.

A few months later, Rabbi Reifer gathered 8 kids

and we once again went to Tchebinia to visit the great rabbi. Again, we left on a Friday to arrive in time for Shabbat, ate dinner and went to the synagogue. The next morning we got up early to go to services. The synagogue was full. We remained all morning. I had learned the service well by this point. After the morning service, they removed the Torah from the Ark and called several people to come up and read from it. After the Torah portion was read, the Torah was replaced in the Aron Kodesh, the Holy Ark. Then the second part of the service, the Musaf, began. After, we returned to where we were staying and it was not until later, after the Havdalah service, that I was again able to wish the great rabbi a "gut Woch," a good week.

The next day when I arrived home, my parents were again happy to see me, asking me about the trip. I thanked my grandfather once more for paying for the trip and he was happy to do it.

I entered the fifth grade in the Polish school. My new teacher was a very strict woman. I continued to study for my Bar Mitzvah with Rabbi Reifer and began to put on Tefillin, the special scrolls in small boxes with leather straps. These are placed in the center of the forehead and on the left arm. When the prayers are finished, the tefillin are put in a special velvet bag. My tefillin bag was given to me by my cousin Esther (Ecia) Lauber.

At 12 years old, I started 6th grade in the Polish school and continued studying for my Bar Mitzvah. I went to my grandfather's house every day, and he would help me, correcting me when I made a mistake. I wrote my Bar

Mitzvah speech on Jewish history, but had to rewrite it several times.

Even after I entered 7th grade, I still made frequent trips to see the Bobover Rebbe. On one trip, I asked him whether I could have my Bar Mitzvah at his synagogue, and he agreed. That trip was particularly memorable, too, because I went and returned home by train.

When I turned 13, I received a letter from the Bobover Rebbe saying that I would have my Bar Mitzvah the following Saturday. To my surprise, my grandfather said that he had already paid for my round trip train tickets

The Reifer family, 1934. Back row, left to right: Leopold, Miriam, Bernard and Alex. Front row, left to right: Manele, Hersh Josef and Chaim.

and for the place where I was to stay. He also wanted to make sure I understood that when a child reaches the age of 13, he becomes an adult and would now be responsible for any wrongdoings he might do.

All week I practiced and practiced. Before I left for the train, my parents gave me a gift of a new, long silk overcoat with a silk hat and silk garterbelt, worn around the waist when one prays in the synagogue. I also received white shirts and new undergarments. I placed everything in my suitcase and was ready for my journey, very excited to be going, and very proud.

In the train I sat down and placed my suitcase on the shelf. A man sat down across from me and said, "You are a Jew," and began to curse me. For the first time, I realized how bad anti-Semitism was in Poland. I tried not to pay attention to this man, but it was difficult. Glad to finally reach my destination, I went to settle in the place where I was staying and practiced a little more for my Bar Mitzvah.

I was so excited that I arrived at the synagogue an hour early for evening prayers. When I told the staff that I was here for my Bar Mitzvah, they wanted me to know me that my grandfather had also paid for a party in my honor Saturday evening, and that the Bobover Rebbe would attend. I was thrilled when I heard this and immediately thanked God and my grandparents for this amazing gift.

The next day, Saturday, came quickly. The prayers began and the Torah was taken out of the Ark. I was the third person to be called up to the Torah, and I felt I did a great job. After the service, when everyone had left the synagogue, long tables with chairs and tablecloths were set up for my dinner party.

The great Bobover Rebbe sat at the head of the table and said the prayers. There were about 100 men seated at my dinner party. When the Bobover Rebbe finished speaking, he let everyone know that the dinner was given by the the honorable Meir Reifer on the occasion of his grandson Iser Reifer's Bar Mitzvah.

I was then asked to give a speech from the Talmud. I began by first thanking the "Toyarah Rebbe" and the rest of the assembled men. "There are differences among the famous sages of the Talmud who make the laws and resolve problems. For example, in the book Bubba Mitziah, two people are holding a garment; one said it belonged to him and the other said it was his. The decision was decided to split the garment."

Another question I spoke about concerned the two groups of sages, Bais-Shamu and Bais-Hillel. The discussion was the following: when a chicken lays an egg on a holy day, may it be eaten? Bais Hillel was of the opinion that you cannot eat this egg. I also spoke about Moses and how he delivered the Jews from slavery. My speech lasted about an hour and everyone seemed pleased. The Bobover Rebbe gave me a kiss and placed his hand on my head and blessed me.

The next morning, I showered and went directly to the synagogue for morning prayers. Afterwards, I visited with the Bobover Rebbe and thanked him for everything. He wished me good luck, and again placed his hands on my head and blessed me.

I went back to where I was staying, thanked my host and left for the railroad station. After a long wait, the train finally arrived, I placed my suitcase above my seat and slept until I arrived in Oswiecim. At the station, I went into the waiting room, bought a drink and took a horse-driven coach to my house. When I arrived, my parents and four brothers were waiting for me outside the house very excited to see me. I told all about my time with the Bobover Rebbe. I didn't leave anything out. I described my speech (pshetel), how happy everybody acted, and how the Bobover Rebbe blessed me. After my mother gave me something to eat, I went straight to my grandparents. I told them about my speech, my "aliya," the call to the Torah, and the blessing I received from the Rebbe. I again thanked my dear grandparents for all they did. I would never forget this fantastic gift. After my grandmother fed me some poppy seed strudel and coffee, I kissed them and left.

In the evening, I went to the synagogue to be with my friends from the Bobover Yeshiva school and to thank Rabbi Reifer for preparing me for the excellent Pshetel performance.

The next day, my father gave me a pack of tobacco called *naipschedniesky* and empty cigarettes. He showed me how to place the tobacco in them and to offer a cigarette to my friends in the synagogue. This was the custom, especially in Oswiecim.

In the morning, my usual routine was to pick up my grandfather and take him to the bathhouse (the Mikve) for his ritual bath, and then bring him back home. Then

I went home to pick up my tefillin and proceeded to prayers. Afterwards, I offered my friends the special cigarettes which I filled with tobacco. Everybody wished me a Happy Birthday and Happy Bar Mitzvah. After my breakfast of two pieces of bread with margarine and an apple which my mother had prepared for me, I went to the Polish school. The teacher also seemed happy to see me and wished me a Happy Birthday. After school and lunch, I went to the Bobover Yeshiva school to continue Talmud study with Rabbi Reifer. When I arrived, everybody was happy to see me and I offered them my special cigarettes. They asked about my speech, and I again told them the entire story about how I had performed on top of a table, and that afterwards the Bobover Rebbe had blessed me. I was the envy of every student from the Jewish school who realized how lucky I was to receive a blessing from the great rabbi.

Three
Working

My father told me that he would like me to do something for my future when I was finished with the seventh grade in the Polish school. I told him that I would like to continue to study, so he suggested that I could continue in the evening and learn business during the day. A few months later, my father spoke to our cousin Shimon Shmeidler, who had the largest haberdashery store in the city, with many salesladies. He asked me to come to his store Monday after school, which I did. I met Mr. Shmeidler, who said I could come to work after class and make some money. I went home and thanked my father.

Several months later, I finished seventh grade and registered for evening class. The following Monday, I started to work in the store. I was introduced to the salesladies. The head saleslady began teaching me how to sell, telling me the names of the items. It took me a long time to learn. I was very polite and the customers seemed to like me, and I was also very good at restocking the items from the warehouse. I was paid every week, and would give the money I had earned to my parents. After several months, Mr. Shmeidler called me to his office and told me that I was getting a raise. I couldn't wait to get home and tell my parents the good news.

After work, I would go to evening school and then pray before retiring. This was my routine for a long time. The only enjoyment was Friday night and Saturday when I took my beloved grandfather to the synagogue, accompanied by my father and four brothers. This was followed by Sabbath meal and songs, after which I would go to the Market Place to play with my friends, where we always had interesting conversations. In the evening, of course, I took my grandfather again to the synagogue for Havdala services, the separation from Shabbat and the rest of the week. The same prayer was said at home by my father, and my brothers and I would help in the singing. On Sunday morning after praying in the synagogue, I went to the Yeshiva, the Jewish school. In the evening, I again met my friends.

I also visited my uncles. Isaac Hutterer, whose wife was my father's sister, had arrived from Berlin, Germany, where he had been an attorney. He had come to Oswiecim with his wife and two children to escape the Nazis. He could not practice law in Poland, so he opened a bicycle store in one of his parents' buildings. He and his family were very nice people and he was successful in his bicycle business. Another uncle was Josef Lauber. He had two children, Iser and Esther, also known as Ecia.

When I was 15 years old, my grandparents invited the

whole family, about 20 people living in our city, over for Passover Seder. This took place in the large dining room. I offered my grandmother help with preparing everything the day before Passover. Every religious family must clean the apartment, emptying it of every crumb of bread, called Boidek Chometz. When the day of Passover arrived, I did not go to work. Instead, I helped my grandmother in the kitchen, helping to make the gefillte fish, peeling potatoes and vegetables, and setting the table. In the evening, I took my grandfather to the synagogue to pray, then went home to wait for the guests. When the whole family was present, my grandfather performed the kiddish, a prayer over the wine. In the center of the table were two large candlesticks with tall candles, and plenty of Matzoh. I helped my grandmother serve the fish, soup, and brisket of beef with vegetables. Dessert was apple compote. After finishing the meal, we sang zmires, songs.

My grandfather gave me the honor of explaining the meaning of Passover.

"I am 15 years old. I thank you, dear parents and especially my grandparents for providing me with the opportunity for my education. Today we celebrate the holiday of Pesach, a tradition of 5695 years, when the Jewish people were slaves in Egypt for 400 years, working 20 hours a day, 7 days a week with no pay. The king of Egypt was the Pharaoh. One day, one of the astrologers told the Pharaoh that he saw in the stars that a male child would be born to the Jewish slaves, who, when he got older, would liberate the slaves. He proposed that the Pharaoh enact a law that all firstborn male children of slaves be killed. So when a baby boy was born to a prominent Jewish family and the mother was afraid the Egyptians would kill her son, she made a basket for the baby, covered it, and gave it to her daughter to place in the river Nile, where the Pharaoh's sister would be bathing. When the Pharaoh's sister saw the basket floating in the river, she asked one of her servants to fetch it and bring it to her. She uncovered the basket, and saw the baby and decided to keep it as her baby prince. She took the child back to the palace and he was brought up as an Egyptian prince, given the best education like the Pharaoh's real son, Ramses. The baby was named Moses, meaning 'from the water.' Moses was most loved by the Pharaoh, who wanted him to be his successor."

I told the rest of the story: how Moses fled to the desert, how he was tending sheep and saw a burning bush. That he obeyed God's command and returned to Egypt. And then the Ten Plagues, and the Exodus of the Israelites.

Several months later, my father spoke to a friend who was the representative of a large company and asked him find me a new job in a different city so that I could gain more experience. After a few weeks, he indeed found me a job in the city of Sosnowice with a religious family named Skochilas, with room and board. I would work in their store selling items to tailors, as well as parts needed for garment manufacturing companies. The week after that I ended my job with my cousin, Mr. Shmeidler. I went home and packed my belongings, and said good night to my four brothers and my parents. The following morning,

I woke up early, took my grandfather on his daily routine, and informed him that I was leaving for Sosnowice for a job and that my brother Lipu would take care of him. After prayers and breakfast, I kissed my family good-bye, took my suitcase and left for the railway station.

In Sosnowice, I was met by Mr. and Mrs. Skochilas, who seemed very nice. They took me to their apartment and showed me my room. I was hungry so they prepared a small meal for me of scrambled eggs with bread and butter. Then we went right away to their small store. They began explaining to me the different items, the names and prices and showed me how to measure (one meter is 100 centimeters, etc.). I learned more each day, and though I caught on fast, it took me a while. I worked 6 days a week. On Saturdays I went to the synagogue with Mr. Skochilas. He paid me every week and I sent the money to my parents.

After several months, I had learned the business quite well and became a professional salesman. Mr. Skochilas began sending me to the city of Bendin to buy merchandise from wholesalers and I brought new customers from the garment industry to the store. Mr. Skochilas told me that I would get a raise in salary. One day I suggested that the store was too small, that we should rent a larger store. After a few weeks, he did just that. I helped transfer the merchandise. Soon, we were even busier that before. I suggested to my boss that he hire help, and he found a lady, whom I trained how to measure and how to serve customers. After a few months, she had learned the business.

I became friends with some of the salesmen for the

wholesalers from whom I bought the merchandise in Bendin. I asked them from whom they bought their merchandise and they said it was from manufacturers in the city of Lodz, and gave me the names of the companies. Upon my return, I told Mr. Skochilas to call them. A few days later the manufacturers called back, and Mr. Skochilas sent me to Lodz. I visited several manufacturers and was able to buy the merchandise for a much cheaper price. I built up the business. My boss gave me an additional raise, all of which I sent to my family. Every couple of months I went to Oswiecim to visit and my parents and brothers were always happy to see me. One of my brothers, however, Manele, was angry at me because I had become less religious and had even cut my side curls. Whenever I returned, I took over from my brother Lipu and brought my grandfather to to the synagogue. I always kept my grandfather informed about my progress as a businessman. He was very encouraged.

Each visit with my family I stayed almost the whole week, and on Sunday went back to Sosnowice to start work again on Monday morning.

I began to make a numer of business trips. I again went to Lodz, but by plane, to buy merchandise in the factories. I stayed in a nice hotel. My boss was very happy that I bought everything for a low price. That year, I made many business trips.

During the two years I worked for Mr. Skochilas, I made a number of friends who were not so religious, and I started to become less observant. One of my customers, a tailor, offered to make a suit for me. This would be my first suit. I had never owned one, always wearing a long overcoat, called a bekishe instead. I decided on a beige fabric, and the tailor made me a perfect suit. When I visited my family a few weeks later, my father became angry because I was wearing this suit and my brother Manele wouldn't even look at me. Since it was Friday evening, I changed to a pair of black pants and a black silk overcoat to go to see my grandparents. They were happy to see me, and I kissed them. They asked how I was, and I told them that I was a good buyer and salesman, which made them happy. I took my grandfather to the synagogue, where everybody looked at me like I was a stranger. After the service, I took my grandfather home and my grandmother invited me to stay for dinner. My grandfather wanted to know what it was that I learned when I went to Lodz to buy merchandise. I told him that I had eliminated some wholesalers, so that profit was higher, and that my boss was completely satisfied with my work.

The following day I returned to Sosnowice, and Mr. Skochilas asked me to go to Lodz to buy more merchandise the very next day. When I arrived at the factory on Lodz, the General Manager there called me to his office and offered me a job as a salesman, selling to stores and wholesalers in all of Poland. I needed to think about it and didn't give him an immediate answer When I arrived in Sosnowice with the merchandise, Mr. Skochilas said that he had received many new orders and that he would like me to return to Lodz right away to buy more. This time, when I came to the factory, I discussed the General Manager's offer, the payment commissions and travel expenses, and he explained how the operation would work. I thanked him again for his offer and left. When I returned to the store, my boss was pleased with the prices I had paid. In the evening, I told my friends about the offer from the factory manager. They suggested that I take it.

A few weeks later, Skochilas again asked me to go to Lodz. I spent three days there, and told the manager that I would take the position of representative. I told him that I could start the following week, after I had quit my present job.

I traveled back to Sosnowice and delivered the merchandise and the next morning, I told Mr. Skochilas that I was quitting. He was very disappointed and tried to convince me to stay, and even offered a substantial raise. But my mind was made up. I thanked him for what he had done for me and set out the following morning for Lodz.

In Lodz, I checked into a small hotel not far from the factory offices. The following morning, I met with the manager, who took me to the showroom and showed me the new sample line. He explained how best to sell the goods, and gave me an order book along with addresses of wholesalers and retail stores. I would receive regular commissions from retail stores and smaller commissions from wholesalers. I would be expected to call on new customers who didn't, as of yet, do business with us. In the order book, I would have to indicate credit details, how long the new customer was in business, the name of his bank, and current supplier. I was told to make clear to each new customer that payment must be made with 30 days. Armed with information, I felt I was ready to begin. I thanked him and left.

The next day, I picked up my samples and went on the road. My first stop was Katowice, where I spent several days visiting the company's current customers and making new contacts.

I also visited my uncle Solomon, my father's brother. In this city, I spoke mostly German, which I had learned by then. The following day I went to Mislovice, then to Chsianov, where I made a few new customers and visited my aunt Pesel, my father's sister, and her husband, who was a wholesaler of men and women's clothing. He gave me several leads for new customers. I began traveling all over Poland, returning to the factory for meetings every four weeks. Every couple of days, I called my parents, so they wouldn't worry about me. I also regularly called my grandfather.

In one of the meetings, the manager explained to the salesmen that many new stores had were been opened all over in Poland by people who had fled Germany. We were told to check every new customer carefully to make sure they were reputable.

The next day, I received my commission; I had done very well.

After several weeks of traveling, I decided to go to Oswiecim to visit my family again. I arrived on a Friday.

I spoke to my father about the rumors that Germany would attack Poland. My father said that my uncle Hutterer, who had fled Berlin and came here, would again run away, because Hitler and his Nazi party wanted to kill all the Jews.

I visited my grandparents that evening. I told my

grandfather how well I was doing as representative, and he asked about my travels and the new people I had met. He was very proud. Later, I took him to the synagogue for services.

My mother had prepared the usual Sabbath dinner, which we enjoyed after the blessing over the wine, the Kiddush. We sang songs and ate. My father inquired about my job, and I let him know that I was doing quite well and traveling to large cities, meeting many people of different nationalities.

I told him a story. Once, I tried to sell something to a religious Jewish school, a Yeshiva, and during the conversation with the buyer, I mentioned that I had attended a Yeshiva. He asked me to quote something from the Talmud, and suggested I start from the part Mishnaies Bruches. I said "Maimesu Corin Shema Bearvis, Beshu Shekohanim Nehnuson Leechol Bitrimuson." He laughed and said that I knew more than he, and invited me to lunch, introducing me to his wife and two children.

The next day, I again took my grandfather to the synagogue, took him back, wished him a Gut Shabbes, and went home to have dinner with my family.

Then, of course, I spend the entire afternoon in the park. Most of my friends had never gone very far and they naturally wanted to know what it was like to travel to so many cities and have conversations with people of different nationalities. I explained that there were many Germans in the city of Katowice, and they hated us. I told them how I had gone to one company, said good morning in Polish ("dzien dobry") but they answered me in German: Guten Morgen. "Guten Morgen," I replied and asked to speak to the manager. I presented my business card and waited. After a few minutes another person came out and asked if I was German. I told him no, that I was Jewish. He look at me with anger and said that they did not buy from Jews. His words were very insulting.

Later, I spoke with my father. He told me that his store was not doing well. There was a lot of competition. I gave him money and said that the following week, I would send more. The next morning, I said good-bye to them all, including my grandparents, and took the train back to Lodz. At the factory, I asked the manager if I could take a extended vacation, to which he agreed. I would keep an eye out for new customers. I received my commission and sent a check to my father. I decided to go to Krinice, the same city that my grandparents had taken me to when I was a young boy. I checked into a hotel and stayed a week, going into the hills and drinking the natural Krinichanka water. I enjoyed the fresh air and visited some stores. Nobody was buying because everyone was convinced the Germans would attack Poland soon.

I decided to stay. I looked for a job and found one in a small, new hotel, as a manager. I organized the front desk and hired new kitchen help and chambermaids. The kitchen was already installed and the chef had his crew in place. Guests arrived daily and after a few weeks the hotel was operating at full capacity. I was working many hours a day, and the owner was very satisfied. Within several weeks, however, the newspapers urgently announced that the Germans were to attack Poland any day. The guests, from many different cities, began checking out. I decided to leave and go home, which upset the owner, but he paid me and I left. I took the train to Oswiecim to be with my family. It was the Summer of 1939.

Four

Invasion

The rumors were everywhere that the Germans would soon attack. Oswiecim was not far from the border. Everybody was buying food. My mother got several loaves of bread and stocked up on non-perishable items for an emergency.

On September 1, 1939, the day we had dreaded finally came. The Germans attacked Poland in a "Blitzkrieg" of tremendous force.

Now there were reports that the German army had orders to kill the Jews in their path. Our family decided to leave. My parents, grandparents, my four brothers and I left by foot with many thousands of other Jewish people. We had no transportation and only bread and apples for food. We decided to go to Lwow, since the city is not far from the Russian border. I remained my grandfather's main source of eyesight as we traveled.

After several days and nights of running, we had finished the bread and apples. I began picking carrots and potatoes from the fields, which we ate raw. When we were very tired, we slept in the fields. My grandparents were exhausted, and rumors swirled that the German army was not far away, and that they were looking to kill Jews.

My family decided that it would be better for them to return to their home in Oswiecim. At least they had friends there.

My grandfather urged me to continue running to the city of Lwow. I kissed my mother, father and brothers. When I kissed my grandfather and said good-bye, he placed his two hands on my head and blessed me. He made a wish that I should live to be 120 years old. He began crying, and I cried as well. I was 18 years old.

I suggested to my mother that I be allowed to take my youngest brother, Hersch Josef, with me. He was only 9. She refused. So we said our tearful goodbyes and I left, giving my father all the cash I still had. It was the last time I was ever with my family.

I continued in the direction of Lwow, together with many hundreds of Jews, mostly young boys and girls. I met a boy from Oswiecim, Leib Klapholz, who I came to call Leon, and we began running together. We ate vegetables from the fields and slept in the wilderness.

After many days of traveling east, we arrived in Lwow, just about the same time that the Soviet Army occupied the city. Leib and I slept in the street for several days, until I met a friend of my father's. I explained that I was alone, that the rest of my family had become tired of running and had gone back to Oswiecim

He asked me if I wanted to make some money. I said of course. He gave me 100 cigarettes and said I should sell them to Russian soldiers. He told me the price, and my share, explaining that in Russian currency 100 kopek is 1 ruble. We arranged to meet the following day. I had successfully gotten rid of all my stock. I met him, gave him the money, and in return, he gave me my profit and an additional 200 cigarettes.

I was very happy. Leib and I immediately went to a small food stand. I bought 2 eggs, baked potatoes, and coffee before going out to sell more cigarettes. I did this for about a week. In the meantime, I had found a room to sleep in and was beginning to learn Russian.

Five
The Coal Mine

I noticed an ad in Polish looking for anybody who wanted to work in Russia, providing registration money in advance. Leib and I went and they accepted us both. They told us to come to the railway station in a few days. When we arrived with our small bags, they put us all together in freight cars, about 30 people in each car. One of the rail cars was a kitchen and the train stopped twice a day so we could be fed. We were provided 800 grams of bread, hot soup and a chance to use the restroom. We slept on the floor and could not wash, except on some stops when we had the opportunity to use the water from the station. Finally, we arrived at the small town of Sorokina. They placed us four in a row and marched us to barracks. Each group of four was put into a small room, with a bed for each of us. They gave us food and told us to assemble in a large room in front of the barracks.

One man spoke to us in Polish explaining that this was the town of the coal mine Shahta 5 Sorokina. We were given some more money and a Propusk, a document authorizing us to enter the large store Uniwermax, where we would not have to stand in line. (In the Soviet Union people had to stand in line for hours in a store.) We entered the store immediately and everybody bought whatever they wanted or needed: soap, toothpaste, sweets, cigarettes and more.

The next day, they showed us the coal mine. Everyone was given the chance to choose the work they wanted to perform. I wanted to know which job paid the most. They said it was called the lav and that it was very dangerous.

The space that I would work in was only 60 inches high at the most and you must roll youself in. They gave me a sled with wheels, head protection and a flashlight. I also received protection for my nose and a coal chopper. They said I should go ahead and see if I wanted to do the job.

I got on my back, rolled and then turned on my stomach. I had only moved several feet and met other people already working. I asked them in Polish how they liked the work, and they said that it was very hard, but that it was true that they did make the most money. I came out and told the supervisor that I would do it. My friend Leon took a lighter job. His job was to dynamite tunnels and then remove the debris.

The room near the kitchen with tables was called Stoloway, which is where they served soup and bread. We slept in our barracks.

The next day, after breakfast, we assembled in the large room. They told us that we would start working the following Monday, and to meet at 8 a.m. in front of the coal mine, when everybody would get the tools to do their job. The workday would last 8 hours, with a one hour break after 4 hours. Access to the mine was by elevator. The mine was operating 7 days a week with three shifts a day. Some weeks I worked the second shift, and some weeks I worked the third shift. Every week, we had one day off.

After several months, I became a professional in the lav and they made me a supervisor to the new arrivals to teach them the basics. The promotion gave me more money. Some days I was working 10–12 hours. I'd shower and change clothes back in the barracks, and go to the Stolowaia restaurant to have some soup and relax. Relaxation meant reading Russian books, so that I began to speak Russian better every day, and I was also learning how to write it. Because there were also many workers from the Ukraine, there were a number of books written in Ukrainian and I began picking that up as well.

One day as I was supervising new arrivals in the coal mine on how to extract coal from the lav, I heard an explosion and people screaming. I came out from the lav and went to where my friend Leon was working. The entrance was full of large stones, and Leon was buried under them. I, along with other people, started to dig him out, which took us a long time, Fortunately, we found him alive. He suffered a broken leg and bruises on his face and body. The ambulance came and took him to the hospital. I spent the night with him in the hospital and went to work in the morning. When the day was done, I visited him again. The doctor had operated on his leg and told me that he would be fine, and although it would take several months to heal, he would have full use of his leg again. He was in a lot of pain, but I was very happy that at least he was alive. I stayed with him the whole night, sleeping in a chair. In the morning, I returned to the coal mine. Every day after work I went to the hospital, and each day he seemed to feel a little better.

Six
Woroshilograd

I had been working in the mines for about eight months when I started thinking that it would best for me to move on. After I determined that Leon would fully recover, I made a decision to leave the coal mine and go to the city of Woroshilograd which is in the Ukraine.

Leon asked me if I had a Propusk, a necessary travel document and of course I didn't, but I insisted that I would go without it.

The train to Woroshilograd traveled at night, so I went to the station with my bundle and waited. It took a quite a while for me to get on the train without anyone seeing me, but I finally managed it. I found a row of seats and crawled under it, staying there for the entire trip.

When the train arrived in Woroshilograd, I waited until all the passengers had gotten off, and then came out from under the seat and went into the waiting room. I found an place near a wall and remained there the whole day and night. The next morning, a lady passed by and asked if I was from Poland. When I said yes, she then asked me if I was Jewish. "Ye," I answered in Yiddish. "Yes." She wanted to know what I was doing in the waiting room. I told her the entire story about working in a coal mine and my friend who had been injured and how I had decided to run away. She offered to take me to her home.

When we got there, she gave me coffee with bread and butter. A short time later, her husband arrived. She introduced me and told him where she had found me. At dinner, the husband, an engineer, asked me from which city in Poland I came. When I said Oswiecim, he let me know that both his parents and his wife's family had also come from Poland. I told him about my background, how I came from a religious family.

They suggested that I stay with them and took me to a room with a bed, where I could rest and shower before sleeping. Breakfast consisted of 2 eggs, bread and coffee. They were very curious about why I had chosen to work in a coal mine and I explained the whole story about how we registered for a trip to the Soviet Union, but were never told where we were going or what work we would perform.

In the evening, a couple of men from the engineering firm joined us for dinner and they asked me what kind of work I did. I was willing to do any type of work. My host said that his wife had a friend who was a manager of a pharmacy and that she would speak to her. Several days later she took me to the pharmacy and introduced me. I was interviewed and the manager told me that I could start working the following day at eight a.m. I thanked him, and the next morning, I filled out the application, which I signed Iser Reifer. By this time, my Russian was fairly good, and I was placed in the lower part of the pharmacy with several other people to place pills in jars (for which I wore plastic gloves), fill spirits in small bottles, and arrange items in the right place. In the evening, my hosts asked me what I did at work, and I told them and that I was very happy to have a job. I thanked them for inviting me to dinner, then asked them for a pen and paper, so that I could write to my family. I had written many letters before and never received an answer.

After working a few weeks in the pharmacy, the manager, Mrs. Alexandra Arkadiewna Misgirowa asked me to have dinner with her in her apartment the next day. That night, I told my hosts not to expect me the next night for dinner. My hosts then allowed me to use their telephone to call my friend in the hospital. He told me that he felt better, and that he had already started walking with crutches. I was very happy to hear that.

The next day after work, I went with the manager to her apartment. She asked me to sit down in the living room and offered me a drink. I had never had anything to drink except for wine during Shabbas or holidays, but I wanted to be gracious. She gave me vodka and Sylodka herring, then served soup and brisket of beef with potatoes, then refilled my vodka glass when she refilled hers. She started the conversation by asking me how I came to Woroshilograd. I told her the story of my life: my family, my childhood, fleeing from the Germans, my family's decision to return to their hometown because the trek was too hard, my constant fleeing because of the rumor that Germans would kill all 18-year old Jews, how I sold cigarettes to Russian soldiers, how I had answered a job ad and end up in a coal mine, how my friend Leon Klapholz was injured in the mine but would recover, how I arrived at the station in Woroshilograd, where a lady befriended me and took me in. "This lady introduced me to you and here I am." Mrs. Alexandra began to cry. She then asked me if I wanted to live in her apartment. I would have to return to the apartment of the nice people who had put me up until then, but I told her that I would move in tomorrow.

After work the next day, I packed my belongings and thanked my hosts again for everything. When I arrived at Mrs. Alexandra's apartment, she was happy to see me and took me to my room, which had a bed, a closet for my belongings, a small table and two chairs. After dinner and saying good night, I went to my room and again wrote letters to my family. My previous ones had never been answered. It was possible that the German government did not allow mail to be delivered to Jews.

Several weeks later, I asked Mrs. Alexandra if I could go and visit my friend in the hospital, and told her that I needed a Porpusk, a travel document. She said that she would prepare the Propusk for me so that I could travel in a few days. I did, and my friend was very happy to see me. He already had begun to slowly move around and said that the doctor thought that in a couple of weeks he would be able to leave the hospital. I told him that I had a nice room in an apartment which belonged to Mrs. Alexandra Misgirowa, and that I would speak to her and ask if he could move in with me. He was very happy. The next day I went back to Woroshilograd. It was already evening when I arrived at the apartment and Mrs. Alexandra asked me about my friend. I told her that he was feeling better and that doctor predicted that he would be released soon. She offered to place another bed in my room, if I wanted to invite him to stay there. Grateful, I called my friend the next day and told him the good news. A few weeks later, I went to pick up my friend. We got to the apartment by bus and when we arrived, Mrs. Alexandra was already waiting with dinner prepared. I introduced Leon and she showed us that she had put a roll-away bed in my room.

The next day, Leon asked me to show him the city after breakfast. We walked around a long time, and my friend liked the city. As we walked past the restaurants, Leon said he would like to work in one. Mrs. Alexandra was preparing dinner as usual, and offered us vodka and herring with some bread. She filled our glasses and said, "Na Zdrowe, to health!" During dinner, she asked Leon what type of work he could do. Leon told her that his father had a butcher store, where he had helped out. Mrs. Alexandra said that she had a friend who was the manager in a restaurant, which happened to be the best restaurant in the city. She told her about Leon and the next day, I accompanied Leon for the interview with the manager, who asked Leon what kind of work he could perform. Leon explained that he had helped his father in his butcher store in Poland. Though the manager was born in Russia, his parents were from Poland and he also spoke Polish. He said that the next day he could introduce him to the chef and that he would start working in the kitchen.

So Leon was introduced to the chef and given a white uniform and a butcher knife. The restaurant received meat by half cows and whole pigs and then separated it into pieces, which Leon already knew how to do. The chef also taught him how to cook and after several months, he received a nice salary. Both the chef and the manager were pleased with Leon and liked him a lot. Leon was very happy with his job and grateful for the introduction to the restaurant manager. When Leon came home to the apartment in the evening, he would always bring home some kind of food, so that we could try his cooking.

Several times a week, I would visit Leon at the restaurant and the manager always spoke very nicely to me. Once, he invited me to have dinner and explained how he became manager and so in return, I told him my story and how I came to be in Russia. He invited me for the next evening and I brought a bottle of spirits, which we soon began to consume slowly. From that day on, he invited me several times a month, and I would always bring a bottle of spirits which I bought in the drugstore. Soon, Leon received a good salary and decided to rent a room. I helped him move and visited him every day.

On February 7, 1941, I turned 20, and Mrs. Alexandra prepared a dinner for me. Leon and her niece Natasha also came. For starters, she served caviar, lox and special bread and vodka, then a mushroom soup, beef brisket with vegetables and a beautiful birthday cake for dessert. We had a wonderful time and thanked her before everybody left after saying good night.

While I lived at Mrs. Alexandra's, I would often call the lady who had found me at the train station and every two weeks or so I would visit her and her husband. They would always ask me if I had heard from my family. Although I often wrote to them, I had not received any answer. It was possible that they had moved. I hoped that they were all right. Our concern was that the German Nazi party under Hitler was the enemy of Jewish people. One of my uncles had been an attorney in Berlin, but when Hitler came to power in 1933, he fled and came to live in Oswiecim with his wife and two children. Another uncle, Ernest Iser Reifer, my father's youngest brother, had been a banker in Vienna, Austria, and when Hitler invaded Austria, he and his family left and eventually came to New York.

When I returned after my visit with these nice people, Mrs. Alexandra asked me what I was interested in doing for my future. I said that I was only interested in working and keeping up with the different languages: Russian, Yiddish, Polish, German and Hebrew.

Seven

Joining the Soviet Army

There were rumors that the Nazis would renege on their treaty with the Soviets, and sure enough, on June 22, 1941, they attacked. It is a date I will never forget. All young men were told to register in the army. There were thousands of us standing in line and it took a long time to reach the registration desk. Leon did not want to register, but I waited with the others and registered in the name of Reifer Israel Berkowitz.

When I told Mrs. Alexandra that I had registered for the army, she stunned and wished me good luck. I phoned the nice lady who had found me at the railway station and the manager of the restaurant, and they also wished me good luck and told me to be careful. Several days later I received a notice to be at the railway station on Tuesday, so I said good bye to Mrs. Alexandra and thanked her for everything she had done for me and my friend. She cried and I too started crying, but I told her that I must go and fight the Nazi army to take revenge for the Jews killed in Poland. The Nazis had taken my whole family away from me and I had to do this.

After many hours on the train, we reached the city of Frunze and were taken in trucks to the barracks. The next day, we received uniforms and they again checked our names and interviewed everybody.

When they learned about all the languages I spoke, they set me aside and told me that I would be placed in a special group, Razwiedka Wiwiad, or Reconnaissance. Training started the following day, and over the next several weeks, I learned how to act on the front, how to catch German soldiers and officers, and became very good at wrestling, judo, karate and martial arts.

Most of the training was at night. Two trenches were dug, divided by 100 to 200 feet. Sticks, visible to us, were placed in the divided area and indicated the presence of mines. In one trench they placed soldiers to watch the other trench.

Our group, Razwiedka, consisted of 10 soldiers with blackened faces and hands. The two soldiers placed in front were GroupA Zahwata, the Catching Group. They were the only soldiers without automatic weapons and grenades, but they were trained in karate and knife-throwing and carried a clasp, a soft ball and knives. Then came GroupA Pricritia, the Covering Group, of 2 soldiers or more. The two soldiers on the left side and the two on the right side were Group Orteza.

In an actual engagement, the engineering group would remove the mines and the Catching Group would move in first, crawling on their stomachs. It was their job to remove any German soldiers, and they were trained to hit the German on the neck with an open hand and then, insert the soft ball in his mouth so he could not scream. Then they would throw him out of the trench to GroupA Pricritia, who would slowly move the prisoner back to our trenches. Once we captured a German soldier, we would be able to interrogate him and learn valuable information about the enemy.

I did very well in the examinations in all the areas and was promoted to sergeant. They placed me, in complete uniform of sergeant, in the Razwiedka Wiwiad, the Reconnaissance group in the 1266 Polka Regiment, 385 Division, WtorohoBielo Rudkoho Front A, the second White Russian Front.

I went to the front with my unit of 10 soldiers, called the Razwiedka Reconaissance, and there we began to counterattack the German army. We traveled day and night by foot for 100 to 200 miles, apprehending and killing several hundreds of German soldiers and officers.

One day, the German army received help from back divisions to prepare trenches for their infantry, allowing them to take cover. The three regiments of our division—1266 Polka, 1268 Polka, and 1270 Polka—reacted quickly by digging trenches and bunkers for the infantry. The staff was very well organized in placing the protection groups, the automatney, Roty, the engineering group, our reconnaissance group, the artillery, the mine throwers, bazookas and the whole fitting division.

It took us several days to establish our observation post and to put our men in place. Every day, I checked their places and the trenches. I also worked with the engineering group to prepare a map of the mines that would protect our front. The mines would be taken out when my Reconnaissance group began moving, but until then, we had to move on our stomachs.

After a few days in the observations posts, I told our officer that we were ready to test the strength of the division and the regiments. The engineering group took out our mines and Atomatney Group had their orders not to shoot, so we began our operation the following night. It was winter, so we had white uniforms with white head caps, special white shoes and white covers for our automatic rifles.

After checking my group one final time, we moved into the trenches. I was in the GroupA Zahwata, the Catching Group, with my best soldier, Boris. He was skilled in martial arts, and I had personally taught him how to put the soft ball into the enemy's mouth. At our right side I placed two soldiers, Group Otreza. On our left, three soldiers, Group Orteza Outcat Group. In the back were four soldiers, GroupA Prycrytia, the Cover Group, and behind them was the Automatney Group, ready to protect us if we had a problem.

When everybody was in place, we began crawling on our stomachs, moving very slowly. We were lucky not to hit a mine. I was the first to step into the German trench, and I hid in a corner while Boris entered on the other side. We waited, hardly breathing, as two German soldiers approached with automatic guns on their backs.

When they were close enough, I hit one of them on the neck and placed the clasp into his mouth. Boris did the same, but the German resisted. Boris used his knife, the only weapon the Catching Group carried, and stabbed the soldier. We both threw our soldiers out of the trench, where GroupA Otreza captured them and took them back to our trenches, stripping them of their automatic guns and grenades. We completed our mission without any losses, and when we all returned to our trenches, we brought two German soldiers to our regiment.

The German soldier who had been knifed was taken to a doctor, so I began interrogating the other officer, asking his name, where he was born, how old he was, and how long he had been in the army. I also asked him the number of his regiment, number and name of his division and where they were located, the name of the commander of the regiment, how many soldiers there were in each battalion and how many battalions in each regiment. He answered many of my questions, so I continued and asked if he was married (yes) and how many kids he had (three).

Through more questioning, I discovered that he had been a member of the Hitler Jugend, Hitler Youth. When I asked him how many Jews he had killed, he just answered that everybody hated Jews. He didn't know why; he just knew he needed to kill them. I then told him that I was a Jew and he begged me not to kill him! I wanted to kill him, but my captain held me back.

The next day, I interrogated the soldier who had been stabbed and got similar answers, except that he had not belonged to the H.J., had English parents and was not married. He asked if I was German, and when I said that

I was a Jew, he was astonished. I sent him to the Shtab division with my interrogation papers.

For this successful operation, I was honored to receive two medals: Za-Otwagu, for bravery, and Otilczny Razwiechyk, for the best Reconnaissance. There wasn't much time to celebrate our success. The next day, at seven a.m., I took my group for one hour of exercise and after breakfast, I sent several soldiers to release the observatory post. My assistant and I returned to the trenches to check them and to prepare for the next operation. We spent the whole day in the trenches, sleeping in our uniforms and shoes and changing guards in front of our bunker every couple of hours. The winter weather made it difficult to check the movement of the German soldiers, but in several days, I was prepared for a large operation.

The observation post told me that there was a large movement on the German side, changing the old division for a new division. I checked for a new location to operate and gave the sketch to our captain. While the engineering department removed the mines, I prepared my group of fifteen soldiers: three soldiers in GrouipA Zahwata, the Catching Group, three in Otreza, three on the right and three on the left, the Outcat Group. I placed the automatic guns group behind the cover of the other groups. My plan was to wait for dark and then attack a bunker on a corner.

After sunset, we emerged from our trench, moving slowly on our stomachs. The Catching Group moved into the German trenches slowly and eliminated the guards. Once inside the bunker, they caught and disarmed two officers, placing soft balls in their mouths and tying their hands. GroupA Pricita, the Cover-up Group, removed the Germans to our side and we all made our way slowly back to our trenches.

The commander was impressed with the success of our operation, and I began interrogating the officers. The first officer had come to the front only 2 days ago and answered all of my questions about his name, service in the army, and his involvement in Hitler Jugend. I continued to ask the usual questions: how many battalions in each regiment, how many regiments in each division, how many people in each battalion, and where on the map the shtab of the regiment was located. He told me that each division held 14,000 soldiers, but he did not know the strength of the artillery.

The next soldier I interrogated was called Dombrowski, who had a Polish father and spoke Polish though he was born in Germany. Continuing the interview in Polish, he confirmed what the first German soldier had said and then added that the German army treated them well. I asked him why the Nazis were killing innocent Jews, and he gave me the same answer as the first soldier: they did not need them! I stood up and told him that I was a Jew and he began to beg for his life. I admitted that I would have liked to kill them both, but I had to send them to the Shtab division. The last thing they said to me was, "Please do not kill us. We have children."

For this operation, I was proud to receive the Order Crasny Zwisdy, the Red Cross, or Red Star. As a reward, we were given vodka.

Eight
In the Soviet Army 1941-1945

With the approach of the summer of 1942, we were given our summer uniforms and were even able to take showers on a nice day. When we came back to our bunker after cleaning up, the officer told us to be prepared, because our 2nd Bialoruske Army would start attacking the German army in a few hours. We started checking the machine guns, the automatic guns, grenades, pistols and special knives.

In the early morning after a few hours of rest, the attack began. We attacked the German front for many days and nights, using heavy artillery and mine throwers. Finally, the German army began to move out, and our division was prepared to pursue them on foot. We ran after them, eliminating several hundred German soldiers and catching many officers. We also confiscated guns, grenades and other arsenal items and captured full trucks of ammunition and heavy tanks.

One night, the Germans stopped running and began to shoot at us from trenches on a reserve station. They were able to hold us off, and that same night, our infantry unit began digging trenches and bunkers not far from the Shtab (Polka) regiment. We rested for a while and the next day began exercising. My assistant and I checked places for the observation posts. I also met with our captain and the engineering group to decide on the location of mines on our side to protect our soldiers. After an entire day of planning, we were ready to place the mines.

I received fresh soldiers for our Reconnaissance Group and started training them at the observation post, although they had been in Wiwiad Reconnaissance. During our karate exercises, I took the two best from the Zahwatam, the Catching Group, and began to prepare them for our upcoming operation. It took several days to teach them the most important aspects of this activity, but they were willing to learn.

Then, the observation post noticed movement in the German trenches and informed me that they were exchanging soldiers. They also observed a new connection from the corner bunker to the trenches, as well as new machine gun stations. I incorporated this information when I gave out the plans for the upcoming operation and trained with my group every day until everyone knew his job.

After a few days, I felt that my group was prepared and informed our captain and the engineering officer, handing them a sketch of the route we would take so that they could take out the mines on our side.

The following night, my group assembled in our trenches. I rechecked everything. Two of GroupA Zahwata, the Catching Group, went over our trenches and slowly moved towards the German trenches. Three Razwieczyks were on the left side, these were the GroupA Otrera, behind them GroupA Prikricia (the Backing Group), consisting of four soldiers. The object was the bunker connected to the trench, and the Catching Group approached and quickly eliminated the guard. Entering the bunker, they captured a sleeping officer, hitting him over the head and placing a ball in his mouth. They passed the officer to the Back Group, and we began moving back to the trenches.

Unfortunately, a soldier on the right side group moved too far to the right and stepped on a mine. The explosion wounded the soldier and also alerted the Germans, who opened fire with machine guns and light artillery. Most of our soldiers were already back on our side, but we managed to rescue the wounded soldier and sent him to the hospital.

I was near the trenches when suddenly something hit me on my right hand, on my little finger. I looked down and saw the blood, realizing that I had been hit by shrapnel. I knew I would have to go to the hospital, but first I had to interrogate the German soldier we had captured.

Though I was in a lot of pain, I carried out the interview, asking the officer the usual questions. He was from Berlin, and I told him that our army would soon be in Berlin. I finished the interview, and like before, when I mentioned that I was Jewish, he begged me to spare his life. I had orders to send him to our Shtab division, but I told him that maybe they would kill him there, since there were also Jews in that division.

When I left the interrogation, I was so furious and in so much pain that I was unable to fall asleep. The next day I saw a specialist at our field office medical center, who told me that my finger was infected. He suggested that my whole arm should be amputated. I told him that he must have been joking, and took out my handgun. I told him that if he wanted to live, he had better take care of my hand. He was shaken, and complied. He knew that I was a top Reconnaissance man, and that I meant business. He took care of me and after several weeks I was able to leave the hospital with a bandage on my hand.

When the hospital released me, I asked to be sent back to the front. They approved my application because of my accomplishments on the front line and the many German officers and soldiers I had captured. A few days later, I was sent to the school at the front. We met in a large hall with many students. The officer of the school, a colonel, read my application and said that he was proud to have me as a student. He had spoken with my division commander, Polpownik Suprunow, and Suprunow had given him the best references on me.

I studied there for several months and graduated first in the class, earning the title Starshyna Staff Feldwebel. I was sent back to the 385th division, but this time I was placed in the 1270 Polka regiment. I was proud to be in charge of training and preparing 45 soldiers for night operations of Nachalnik Razwiedki Polka. I was also pleased to be working with Captain Goncharow, head of the Reconnaissance regiment; Major Kuznicow Pomochnik, Commander of the Polka regiment and Pukownik Halin, the Shtab Polka assistant of the Nachalnik of the regiment.

We trained for two hours every morning, took a break to eat some soup and bread, and then continued training. At night, my assistant and I went to the trenches to talk to the observation post soldiers, who gave us information about bunkers and machine gun locations near the trenches.

I gave out the information from the observation post and started making preparations, which I submitted to our Towarish (friend), comrade Captain Goncharow, who in turn showed it to comrade Polkownik Chalin, the head of our regiment. When we received the OK, I brought a sketch of our operations to the engineering department so they could take out the mines in the area.

Soon thereafter, the two best soldiers of the Catching Group, Schipiokin and Bannikow, started moving on their stomachs toward the German trenches. They carried knives, clasps and two grenades each as they approached the bunker. On the right was GroupA Otreza, and on the left, the Outcat Group, consisting of two soldiers. The four Reconnaissance soldiers of the Catching Group were in the back.

The Catching Group entered the German trenches and carefully moved to the bunker. Eliminating the two guards in front, they entered the bunker and found three soldiers and one officer. The soldiers were killed but they took the officer prisoner. They handed him over to the Groupa Pricitia, the Cover-up Group. On the way back, I noticed that one of our soldiers had moved too far to the right and I heard an explosion. He had detonated a mine, which wounded him in the leg and the stomach. Germans immediately started shooting at our group with automatic weapons.

The wounded soldier and our additional casualties were taken to the field hospital, while the German officer was taken to the ShtabPolka regiment to be interrogated. He was nervous, but he answered all my questions and gave us valuable information.

I began with the basic questions and learned that he had been born in Vienna, Austria, had a wife and three children, and had been in the army for two years. He had been transferred from the artillery when they found out that he drank too much. His regiment received food every couple of weeks and was allowed to go to town for alcohol. However, the artillery was in trouble, since they were not receiving sufficient ammunition. He also told me the location of the Shtab of his regiment and of his division, and listed the names of the officers. The infantry were new recruits, he said, except for the machine gun operators, and there were many reservist soldiers in the small towns.

As I had done before, I revealed that I was Jewish, and the officer asked me not to kill him. I was under orders to send him to the Shtab division, but before I did, I told him about my uncle who had once lived in Vienna. However, when Hitler took over Austria, my uncle was forced to flee his home and eventually moved to New York.

We had several successful operations in 1943, but there were still casualties and we sent many soldiers to the field hospital. We visited our wounded soldiers often to comfort them and give them courage during their recovery. When they were released from the hospital, we took them back and gave them an inside job.

Whenever I was in the Reconnaissance operations, I never thought of my life as in danger. I always told myself that if the Germans ever caught me, I would commit suicide. I was just happy to be able to contribute to the fight against the Nazis and to eliminate as many German soldiers as I could.

Whenever I interviewed Germans caught in the field, I always made a point to tell them that I was a Jew and they would beg me not to kill them, even though the Nazis were killing millions of innocent Jewish families. This, I would tell my comrade soldiers, was the nature of our enemy. The Nazis had attacked our Russian country, killing families and children and burning our cities, factories and farms. For years, they had been sending innocent people to the gas chambers and then to crematoria. They destroyed everything. I reminded my soldiers not to have mercy on these Nazi animals, because if we did not kill or capture them, they would kill us and anyone else in their path. The Nazis were not human; they were worse than any wild animal. I constantly reminded my comrades that we had to fight for our land.

In the winter of 1943, we were in the Smolensk Oblast. It was bitterly cold, but still our army attacked the German army with everything we had, including heavy artillery, heavy mine throwers, planes and machine guns. It was thundering all day and night. The Germans started moving back, and our army pursued them. It took several days, but we eliminated many of them.

At one point, the German army had backed up and prepared trenches for the running soldiers and bunkers. Our GroupA Razwiedki Reconnaissance was near the ShtabPolka regiment, and we started building bunkers and preparing observation posts while the infantry readied machine gun replacements, minamiot mine thrower stations and light artillery stations.

We prepared our white uniforms and exercised the following morning after breakfast. In the evening, Captain Goncharow called me to his bunker and told me that the Germans had a new division facing ours. After checking with the observation posts and the engineering department, I told him I'd be ready in a few days.

We began practicing the following day. It was freezing outside, but we persevered for several hours. After some hot soup and 800 grams of bread to warm us up, we rested a bit until evening, when we would practice again. We began to carefully move on our stomachs and to move the hand grenades from the front to the back. To avoid accidents, we all covered our heads with white caps and part of our faces with some white material.

I arranged the group in the usual order and advised Captain Goncharow that we were ready. I brought him the layout sketch to give to the engineering group, and said that I could begin the operation the following night.

Goncharow told me that Captain Nosow, the assistant to Major Kuznitsew Nathalnik of Shtaba regiment, desired to go with me. I was hesitant, because the mission would be very dangerous, so at Captain Goncharow's advice I went to the second bunker to talk to Captain Nosow. Once I was sure that Captain Nosow would follow my orders during the operation, I told him to meet me the following evening in the trench near bunker #4, in a white uniform. Then I checked on the layout one more time.

When it began to get dark, we assembled near bunker #4. It took two hours for the mine group and the engineering group to remove the mines on our side. Then, Schypiotkin and Morozow of the Catching Group began moving on their stomachs. There were four soldiers in Groupa Pricritia, (the Cover-up Group). Groupa Otreza, the Right Outcat Group, consisted of two and the left Outcat of two soldiers. I was on the right side of the Outcat group and Captain Nosow on the left.

Group Zahwata moved slowly on their stomachs to the front of the bunker, where they hit the sleeping guard over the head and placed a sponge ball in his mouth, the clasp. They tied his hands and threw him out to the cover-up group. I left the center group and moved the prisoner to our trenches.

However, Captain Nosow moved to the wrong side and stepped on a mine, triggering a strong explosion. Some of my soldiers were already in our trenches with the captured officer, but the Germans began shooting with machine guns and light artillery. I moved to Captain Nosow's side and saw that the explosion had wounded him on both legs. Taking his two hands, I removed him to our trenches, where he and three other wounded soldiers were transferred to the field hospital.

Meanwhile, I interrogated the German officer we had captured. He was a captain and said that the name of the general of his division was Felker, quite famous, of the 27th Army Corps. Usual questions about Jews followed.

When I visited Captain Nosow and the soldiers, they were all in bad shape. The doctor informed me that both of Captain Nosow's legs required amputation, which was performed the next day. I was very upset to hear this.

The next day, I got more personnel and began preparing them for work. Luckily, they learned quickly, and we had several more successful operations.

In 1944, Captain Goncharow was promoted to Major and I was promoted to Lieutenant. I was also honored with the Order Crasny Znameni. Although I had already received many orders and medals during the war, this order signified the elite of the Russian army. Our Division Commander Polkownik Supronow received the title of Major General, and he held a party in celebration with me, Major Kuznitsew, and many of the other officers. Major Goncharow and I celebrated my successful operations in the Reconnaissance, touching glasses and saying, "Nazdrowie, to health!"

The night was filled with celebrations and congratulations, but after half a day's rest, I knew I had to begin working on my future operations. In addition to identifying the general of his division as General Felker, the last German officer we had interrogated had pointed out a large bunker on the map where he said the general slept. It was in a nearby town, not far from the frontlines. He claimed that he knew this because he had been summoned by the general along with several other officers to be interviewed as assistants in the general's quarters, although he was not chosen.

At the end of 1944, the German division in front of ours was small, and did not act as the previously encountered divisions did. We saw very little movement in their trenches. In some spots, the trenches were empty; they had lost many soldiers through our attacks, and now they were waiting for reinforcements and ammunition.

Checking the observation posts, I planned the operation, laying out the route from our trenches to the small town where General Felker's bunker was located. I knew that we would meet many guards, but I hoped for the best. I had always been a gambler when it came to our front against the Nazis. Goncharow checked my plan and considered it very risky and I promised to be very careful, but it would take me a week to prepare. He said that he would show my plan to Pulkownik Halin and if he thought we needed permission from Major General Suprunow it would take several days.

In the meantime, I organized my groups. I had four of the best soldiers from Reconnaissance: Schypiotkin, Bannikow, Morozow and Karl. Then there were two soldiers in Orteza, two in Prikritia and ten soldiers with automatic machine guns in the trenches in the back. We trained all day and all night, building a large bunker with several soldiers inside and others as guards outside and in front of the bunker.

Finally, I received a reply from Goncharow, but it was not what I had expected. He thought my plan was too dangerous, and he did not want to lose any Reconnaissance in such a risky operation. They would give the layout of the operation to the artillery and the aviation group. The next day, I told my group that Major Goncharow, Commander Polka, and Pukownik Halin did not approve the mission.

On the German side, movement was observed: a possible change of soldiers to a new division. I spoke to Goncharow and he told me that our artillery and mine throwers with heavy machine guns would begin a night operation. Nobody slept that night. It was thundering with artillery, minamotin, machine guns and small hand rifles. In the morning, it was quiet in the trenches. When I checked our observation post, I was told that the Germans put out more machine gun stations and many soldiers were moving back and forth in the trenches. Before planning this new operation, I had to know if the new German soldiers occupied the same bunkers, or if they had made new ones.

We observed the German movements every day until finally we were ready. This time, there would be two from Reconnaissance Group A, Zachwata, four from GroupA Otreza, and four from GroupA Prycriytia, and me, totaling 11 Reconnaissance. Some in the group were new Reconnaissance soldiers from different divisions who had come to us after being released from the hospital for various injuries. I took my comrades every day for training in the front trenches.

My plan, which I presented to Major Goncharow, was to approach a small bunker connected to a small trench on the right side. One night, Goncharow came with us to the trenches. There we were, ready to carry out our operation. Though there were many guards in front of the bunker, I decided to gamble and try to capture the officers.

The engineering group took out the mines, and then our group slowly moved on their stomachs towards the bunker. The Catching Group hit the soldier guarding the bunker in the back of the neck, sticking the soft ball into his mouth and killing him with his knife. The two German soldiers found in the bunker were met with the same fate. We also found two officers sleeping, a lieutenant and a sergeant. The sergeant was killed, but we disarmed the lieutenant and removed him without any hassle. Moving back to our trenches, one of our men moved too far to the right and stepped on a mine, blowing off part of his right hand. This alerted the Germans, and they began shooting. I rushed to the injured soldier to remove him. The German officer was already in our trenches.

We brought the captured officer over to our Shtab and I interviewed him in front of Goncharow: name, age, two kids at home, weeks on the front, teaching new recruits. I learned that there was a shortage of recruits and that his division was mostly made up of new recruits with no experience. He showed me the position of his shtab division on the map, saying that the position of his division had not been good since the Russian offensive into Germany. I told him that we were winning the war.

When I asked about his membership in the Hitler Youth, he answered affirmatively, but refused to say how many Jews he had killed. When I told him I was Jewish, he had the same reaction as other German officers: begging to be spared. As before, I said that I would not kill him, and sent him to our Shtab division.

After a few days of rest, we checked the front trenches at night. Speaking to our soldiers and officers, I learned that the Germans were retreating slowly, and I tried to find out how strong they were. I took a few comrades, friends, and worked the same way as previously. I was again successful and brought back an officer and a soldier without any losses on our side.

The officer I interviewed said that his division was in bad shape, running out of supplies and ammunition. They were talking about the success of the Russian army in taking Poland and entering Germany, and they did not see any future in continuing to fight.

After the interrogation, I visited my wounded comrade at the hospital and he was happy to see me. His arm was better, and he had even written a letter to his family. I wished him good luck before I left.

1944 was a tough year, but our 385th division was very

successful. At the end of 1944, we were nominated as the best division in our 2nd Bialoruskoho army, Front A, and received the name 385 Krychowskaia, Krasnoznamionaia Orden Sunworowa Division.

Our army was moving forward and continued to pursue the Germans, apprehending thousands of soldiers and officers, taking away their guns and ammunition and transferring them to the back of the front.

In 1945, we moved in the direction of Berlin. Over several months, we overtook many towns and cities until at last we came close to the city. We approached the famous Reichstag. And on May 4, 1945, the same day that Hitler and Eva Braun committed suicide and his associates burned the corpses, I was promoted to captain and received a medal, Za Pobiedu Nad, for winning the war. I also received the medal Za Stalingrad for previous operations.

After I was transferred to the city of Grabow, not far from Berlin, I was promoted to be the adjutant to the commander of Grabow, Colonel Pulkownik Koshelow, who had known me for many years. When I came to introduce myself, he said, "I am happy to see you alive."

"Likewise," I replied.

The next day I scheduled a meeting with the mayor of the city. When we met, I introduced myself and spoke to him in German, and he thought at first that maybe I was German. at first. I wanted to know about the situation in the town, and said the mayor told me that Grabow was not too badly damaged and already in the process of restoration. When I asked about the police force, he explained that the police had to remove the swastika from their uniforms, and that all of Hitler's and other Nazi signs and statues needed removal at once.

After the mayor left, I spoke to the colonel and suggested emptying the buildings across from the Komendatur to create a center for people who were still alive, those not killed by the Nazis in the concentration camps, and who were in transit through the city. The colonel agreed. The following day I told the mayor that I wanted to take the building across the street and build a kitchen with bedrooms, and provide clothing for the men and women who had been liberated from the concentration camps. The people living in the building were told to leave, and within a very short time the place was ready for the refugees, with a chef ready to feed them. I put up a sign announcing, "Transition Place."

Nine

Meeting the American Army

The following day, the colonel told me to go the city of Ludwigslust, where the American army was located. We were to meet the officers and introduce ourselves as neighbors.

Ludwigslust was not far. At the entrance to the small city, I met American soldiers. I said hello, but I did not speak English. Speaking in Russian, I told them that I was the adjutant to the Commander of Grabow.

One of the soldiers seemed to understand me a little and when I realized he spoke Polish we were able to continue the conversation. His name was Stanislaw Runicky and his parents had left Poland for the United States before he was born. I told him how I was born in Poland and that when Germany attacked Poland in 1939, I had to leave my hometown, eventually joining the Russian army in 1941. He introduced me to the Americans. Along with Stanislaw, who was from Michigan, there was Jerry Adler from New York, Sergeant White from New York, and Mac Allen from Mississippi. We took a group picture.

May 5, 1945. Reifer (third from left) with American officers

With Runicky translating, I expressed how glad I was to have met them, and then I then asked them for a favor. I told them that I had an uncle in New York and wanted to send him a letter letting him know that I was alive and in the Russian army. They agreed to help and I planned to bring the letter the next day.

I learned that Jerry Adler was Jewish, and understood a little Yiddish because his father spoke it. I wrote the letter in Yiddish in the hopes that Adler's father could read my instructions and that my uncle would know that it was truly his nephew. This is a translation of the letter I wrote to my uncle:

My dear uncle,

I am letting you know that I am an officer in the Russian army and I met the son of Mr. Adler in the city of Ludwig-

slust, Germany and through him I am sending you this letter.
I was fighting the German Army from 1941 until the end of
the war. I was in the Reconnaissance, an officer, and I killed
many hundreds of German soldiers. I hope to go to Oswiecim
in a short time and hope to see my family, my parents, grandparents, brothers. And of course, I hope to also see you, my
aunt Friedl, your daughter Mary and son Hans. Best regards
to all.

Your nephew,

Alex Reifer

The next day, I gave Runicky the letter so that he
could pass it along to Adler, who promised to forward
it along to his parents. Hopefully, they would be able
to find my uncle, Ernest Iser Reifer. I knew he lived in
New York, but I did not know the address. I knew that
New York was a big city, but maybe my uncle had kept
the same name he had in Vienna. We took more pictures
and they invited me for a drink.

Ten
Transition Place

I explained to Runicky that I had arranged with the mayor of Grabow to clean up the building across the street from the Komendatur and create a transition place for people who survived the concentration camps. This Transition Place would operate 24 hours a day, with a kitchen to provide plenty of food and necessary clothes to anyone who survived. The sick would be transferred to the hospital. All this was worked out with the mayor, who had promised that everything would be supplied. He even sent a woman to be a manager for the Transition Place. I told him that the Nazis evicted the Jews from their homes, letting them starve. The healthy Jews were put to work in the camps, and the sick, the old and the children were gassed and cremated, unless they had already died of starvation.

For the first few days, several hundred people passed through the place. I asked the Colonel to come and see the place. He was astonished at what I had done, and when we returned to the Komendatur across the street, he thanked me. I told the Colonel that I had visited the Americans and that some of them wanted to see Transition Place. He told me to bring them.

The next day, Stanislaw Runicky and Jerry Adler came to visit the Transition Place. They were able to observe how a bakery truck unloaded bread and how people were lined up in the kitchen for their soup and bread. Then I brought them over to the Komendatur and introduced them to the Colonel before we had some drinks of vodka.

A few hours later, I went back to the Transition Place and saw some people looking like skeletons standing in line in the kitchen. They were survivors of concentration camps. I spoke to some of them and learned they were from many different countries: Poland, Czechoslovakia, Romania, Holland, Belgium and France. Most of them said they wanted to go to the United States.

I noticed two girls in line asking the server if they could have more soup, which they were given. When I spoke with them, they told me that they were from Paris, France, and that they wanted to go home. I offered to take them to the American side, which they were very happy to hear. I told them to pick up some dresses and that I would meet them the next day.

When I arrived, there were more people ready to leave. Upon my return to the Komendatur, the Colonel was pleased with what I had done for the girls.

Most of the people in the Transition Place were Jewish. I introduced myself to many of these survivors, telling them that I also am Jewish, the Adjutant to the Colonel and the organizer of this Transition Place. My duties at the Transition Place kept me very busy and I worked many hours a day, but I was not tired. I knew that I was doing something for my people, and maybe someday someone would do the same for my family. When I visited the Americans again, Runicky had already told them about the Transition Place in Grabow for those liberated from the death camps and what was available for the survivors there. They thanked me for my efforts and we drank whiskey.

On May 9, 1945, the Colonel and I were invited to the Komendatur in Berlin to celebrate the declaration of the end of the war. I was proud of my efforts during my five years in the Russian army and of all the decorations I had earned. As a captain, I was respected by those celebrating our victory over the Germans.

The Commander of the city of Berlin approached me, holding two glasses of vodka. We had known each other for a long time, and he handed me a glass to make a toast, saying, "Nazdrwsie, to health!" We talked for a bit, and then he found me again an hour later, filling my glass again and toasting, "Za pobiedu nad germanie, for winning the war over Germany!" Before leaving, Pulkownik and I approached the table of the Commander of Berlin, General Kotikow, and thanked him for the invitation to the party. I said "Doswidania, see you again!"

The war was over but there was still much work to be done in Grabow. Whenever I went to the Transition Place, and looked at the hundreds of people, skeletons, some walking with canes, some very slowly, I had to go back to my room for a glass of vodka and cry myself to sleep. It hurt me so very much to watch these poor people, on the floor of their rooms, sleeping or just sitting there.

I started a conversation with one of them in Russian and he answered me in Polish. When I then spoke Polish, he wanted to know if I was a Pole. I said yes, but added that I was also a Jew. He had come to the Transition Place after surviving the camp in Auschwitz, and I told him that I was born in that city. I learned that the Nazis had deported all the Jews from the city and sent them to Sosnowice.

He then told me more about Auschwitz, and how he had lost his entire family in the crematorium. The Germans took the old, the sick, the children, anyone who could not work and sent them to the gas chambers, and then to the crematoriums, which were operating 24 hours a day. Other people told me that the Nazis made them work in the gas chambers, which they called showers, to remove the bodies and put them into the crematoriums.

When I listened to these mostly young people explain how the Nazis treated them, I almost couldn't believe it until I looked at their faces. They were told that they would be safe if they continued to work, and that if they stopped working they would end up in the same crematorium as their families.

When I heard all of this, I had to go back to my room to drink a glass of vodka and try, unsuccessfully, to sleep. I knew that I would never forget the hatred of the Nazis and the millions of innocent men, women and children they had murdered. It was horrible to think that they built gas chambers and crematoriums right next to the city in which I was born and lived until I was 18 years old. More people arrived at the Transition Place every day, and I worked diligently to accommodate them. I found several men to volunteer in the kitchen and prepared two more rooms on the second floor for storage of garments, since we received second-hand clothes several times a week from the city.

When I met with the mayor and our colonel, I pleaded for more food and clothing to help with the increasing numbers of people who came to the Transition Place and wanted to go over to the American side. I told them what the survivors had said about the concentration camps and offered to show them pictures. The mayor said that he could not believe that Germans could do such a thing. I knew that although the German people were intelligent, but when Hitler came to power in 1933, and organized the Hitler Youth, the Gestapo and the SS, his policy was to eliminate the Jews and to wage war. He wanted to control Europe, Russia and the whole world.

In the Transition Place, everything was going well. I made a sign for the front: "The Holocaust Survivors' Transfer Place." When I spoke to some people from Lodz, one survivor told me how the Gestapo took several thousands of Jews to the center of town and then separated the old people and the small children from the rest, shooting them with machine guns right in front of the others. Among those that were killed, the survivor said, were his parents and two youngest brothers. The Germans made younger, healthy Jews place the bodies on trucks to be taken away to be disposed of and then they took them to the camps to work. They worked day and night and were allowed to sleep only a few hours, in rotten garments with their shoes on. For rations, they received a small piece of bread. There was no hospital to treat those that became sick. They were just taken away and never seen again.

Those who were liberated were referred to as Survivors, and I often listened to their stories. I heard how the Gestapo, the SS and other Germans treated the Jews: always insulting them, calling them dirty Jews, and beating them for no reason other than that they were Jews.

All the Jews who passed through the Transition Place were lucky to be alive and I was happy to be able to prepare for them and help them. It was a joy to see surviors from Poland, Czechoslovakia, Belgium, Holland, France and several other countries when they were reunited with relatives and were able to leave together.

I learned that hate only destroys people. I feel that we need to teach our children to be friendly and to not to be against each other. Even though it will take a long time, we must start. In the Talmud, our sages wrote "do not kill," "do not hate," "do not steal," "do not lie," and "respect your neighbor, and if you can help him, do it." Today, the majority of countries in the world hate each other, begin wars and kill innocent people and children. But I will always remember nice people, Jewish and non-Jewish, who helped me when I was in bad shape.

I often wondered about my family, where they were and what they had endured. In June of 1945, I finally received a response from my uncle in New York. This is a translation of his letter.

Dear Iser,

You cannot imagine how happy you made me to let me know that you are alive and that you are in the Russian Army! I am so very proud of you, you belong to a country that are heroes of the world and protect the world from destruction. In short, I can tell you that my family and I fled Austria through France, North Africa and Portugal to finally arrive in America. We are all healthy. The Nazis deported our entire family from Oswiecim to Sosnowice. I received a letter from your father in October 1941, but after the United States entered the war we could not receive any more letters from Europe. I am giving you the address of our family in Oswiecim and in Sosnowice, so that you can find out what happened to them. Remember to be in contact with me all the time. At this time, you are the only one left of our family. I would like you to take revenge on the Nazis who killed many millions of Jews. I love you.

Best regards from my family,

Your uncle.

During my five years of fighting the Germans in the Reconnaissance, whenever I caught a German officer or soldier and asked him why he killed Jews, the only answer was: "because they are Jews." After all of my questions I would let them know that I was a Jew and every one of them would stand up and beg me not to kill him. I could not undo the horrible things the Nazis had done to the Jewish people, but being able to fight against the army that had destroyed my family was my satisfaction.

In December 1945, I went back to the Central Komendatur in Berlin for a New Year's party held by General Kotikow. I attended with my colonel and we brought a case of our Russian vodka as a present. The party lasted all night. Caviar was served with Sylodka-Herring, salmon steak with vegetables and sweets for dessert. We all celebrated the New Year with Russian songs and many glasses of vodka. I do not recall how many glasses I had, because I fell asleep. The following morning, we returned to our Komendatur, where I was able to take a shower and get some rest.

Eleven
Return to Oświęcim

In early 1946, I asked Colonel Pukownik Koshelow for a two-week vacation to visit my hometown of Oświęcim. I was hoping to find out what happened to my family. The Colonel called for a Propusk, a permit to travel to Poland, which I received the following day. I made my reservations and several days later, I was ready for my trip. At this point the Transition Place was very slow, because many people had just passed through. I asked my assistant to take care of the Place.

I took the plane from Berlin to Warsaw and then on to Krakow. From there I continued to Oświęcim. Soon after registering in a hotel, I went to the building where I had lived with my family. Along the way, I spoke to several people who told me that the Germans had sent all the Jews to Sosnowiec.

The next day, I visited the concentration camp, with the gas chambers and the crematoriums. Seeing all this, I began to cry. How could these barbaric people, the Nazi

SS and the Gestapo, torture innocent people and little children and then burn their remains in the crematoriums? Back at the hotel, I managed to eat something, but I was still filled with stress and nervous tension. I went to the bar for a few vodka drinks. I started a conversation with with the Polish people there, and when I told them I was Jewish, they looked at me in disbelief. They thought that Hitler had killed all the Jews.

As the conversation continued, I realized that Polish anti-Semitism was just as strong as before the war. I was so angry I thought I might kill someone, so I left the bar before I could act on my anger.

In the center of town, I recognized several Polish policemen from the time I had attended the Polish school. They confirmed that the Germans had taken all the Jews to Sosnowiec. I knew that Oświęcim had once had 7500 Jewish families and 4500 Christian families. On Saturdays, the entire city closed down for the Sabbath.

The next day, I checked out of the hotel and went out to meet people. I passed the street where I had worked for Mr. Skochilas, but now the store was closed and the entire street was in bad shape. I ran into several people who recognized me and called me by my name of Iser. They wanted to know how I became an officer in the Russian army, so I told them how I fought the German army and received many decorations for my successful operations. I also told them that I was now the Adjutant to Colonel Pukownik Koshelow, commander of the city of Grabow in Germany.

I asked them to tell me if they knew where my family was, since I had come there in the hope of finding them but had been unable to find anyone. A girl came up to me and said that my cousin Ecia Esther Eckstein was alive. Even though she did not know exactly where she was, I was overjoyed to hear that someone from my family had survived.

The girl suggested that someone named Mala Tauber might know where my cousin could be found. Mala and the Tauber family had lived not far from our home in Oświęcim and I had gone to the Jewish school with Mala's brother. She told me Mala's address in Sosnowiec and I immediately traveled there. Mala was very pleased to see me, but had a problem. Could I help? Her boyfriend, a concentration camp survivor, had been arrested and was now in jail in Katowice, a nearby town. She hoped I could get him out, and I promised that I would try.

The following day, I went to Katowice with Mala Tauber to see the Police Commander. Fela waited outside while I went in and asked the Lieutenant at the front desk to see the Commander.

After a minute, the Commander came out and asked what he could do for me. I told him that I had been fighting the Germans for five years on the front, which he could see because of my decorations. I explained that when I came home to search for my family, I found out that one of my cousins, was in jail after being in a concentration camp for 5 years.

The Commander had my "cousin," I'll call him Solomon, brought in and asked if this was indeed my cousin. I said yes, and the Commander ordered his lieutenant to prepare him for immediate release.

They took Solomon to the back and in the meantime the commander asked me how I had received so many decorations. I told him about my time in Reconnaissance, how we caught many hundreds of German Nazi officers and took the Reichstag in Berlin. While we waited for Solomon, I showed him pictures from Lugwigslust and told about how I was the first Russian officer to meet the American 82nd division before the end of the war in 1945. He saluted me for my courage and ambition, and said that he was very sorry that I had lost my family.

Auschwitz: Prisoner Barack Type 260-G

facing page: Barracks perimeter of Auschwitz, 1945

Soon Solomon came out and stood next to me as the Commander handed me the release papers. I saluted the Commander and thanked him for releasing my cousin. Solomon said he had a suitcase, which I asked the Commander for. It was brought to us and we left.

Outside, Mala embraced Solomon. I gave her the suitcase, but he told her to leave it with me. I was returning to Germany, so I gave him my address there so that he could come and pick up the suitcase in a few weeks. On our journey back from Katowice, they thanked me many times and peppered me with questions until we reached Sosnowiec.

I continued on the train to Oświęcim, and after I checked into a hotel and ate supper, I had my vodka and went to sleep. The next day, I went again to see the concentration camp and crematorium and took some pictures.

The next day, I called the airport to fly back to Germany. I changed my jacket, as I did not travel with the jacket that displayed my decorations. I checked out of the hotel, taking the suitcase along with my own, and left for the airport. The flight made several landings: Krakow, Warsaw, Berlin and finally Grabow. I arrived at my apartment, where I took a drink of vodka and fell asleep. When I awoke several hours later, I unpacked my belongings, hung them up and put Solomon's suitcase under my bed.

When I came to the Komendatur, the Colonel was very happy to see me. He asked if I had found anyone from my family. I told him that I had not, and that I found out that the Germans sent the Jews to the concentration camp, where they were sent to a shower, which was really

Auschwitz, 1945

a gas chamber. There they were killed and their remains were burned in the crematorium. I told him that I believed that my mother and father, as well as my four brothers, were sent to their death like this. The colonel was truly sorry to hear about my loss.

I went to my office to check my mail, then I called the mayor and left a message telling him to come and see me. I went to check on the Transition Camp and realized that there were still many people passing through. Many were very weak and stayed until they recovered.

I told them that they should be happy to be alive and that I believed that they would be successful in the future and have a good life. I also said that it is very difficult to forget the past but that they should remember

Auschwitz: Stockpile of victims' glasses

that the Jewish people are resilient, ambitious and always eventually succeeded.

Every day I spent several hours with the new arrivals, and listened to the terrible stories of what they had to go through. I told them that I just returned from a trip to the city of my birth, Oświęcim, and that I did not find any member of my family alive. Many of the people I spoke to told me about the concentration camps and all I could think of was how I lost my parents and four younger brothers.

I wrote to my uncle Reifer in New York and asked him to find the address of my uncle Feiner, my mother's brother who had a factory, Ash-Can Company.

I again went to Ludwigslust to meet the American officers and soldiers to ask them to send my letter to my uncle Reifer in New York. They promised to send it and then we went for lunch. They served whiskey called Chivas Regal, which was very good. I thanked them for sending the letter and for lunch, and then I went back to my office in Grabow.

I worked until 5, and stopped after supper at the Transition Place. When I checked the kitchen, the cook told me that he was going to be short of vegetables and rice, so I called the mayor to tell him. He said that he had already ordered them and that they would be delivered that day, for which I was grateful.

Often, I would work so many hours and be so tired in the evening after checking the Transition Camp that I would retire to my room, have a glass of vodka, and go to sleep without eating supper.

When I was working in my office the next day, my assistant came in and said there was someone asking to see Captain Reifer. I came out a few minutes later and found Solomon. I invited him into my office, and we sat down and talked. Mala was fine, he told me and they hoped to be married soon. I wished them good luck. Then he asked me about his suitcase, and I told him to come back the next day around noon to pick it up.

In the evening when I went back to my apartment, I took the suitcase out from under my bed and opened it. I was shocked to find that the suitcase was filled with German money, 50 and 100 Reichmark bills. They must have been taken directly from a bank, because of the way they were bundled. I had never had the experience of seeing that much money.

But then I closed the suitcase and placed it back under the bed. Personally I was not interested in money, because in Russia one does not need German marks. In my future in Russia, all I needed to do was to study for higher ranks to go as high as I could go.

The next day, I took the suitcase with me to the office, and when Solomon came at noon, I gave it to him. He thanked me and I told him to be careful. Maybe he understood what I meant.

I went back to work, making calls. I began to write another letter to my uncle in New York. I asked about his wife Friedl and his children Mary and Hans, and whether or not he had found my uncle Feiner. I also wrote that I was planning to ask my colonel for a transfer to the Polish army, with recommendations, since I was born in

Poland and lived there until the age of 18. The next day, I went to Ludwigslust to give Stanislaw Rudicky my letter, so that it could be forwarded.

I walked into the Colonel's office and said that I had something important to ask him. He told me to go ahead, so I began:

"I have been serving in our Russian army and fighting the Germans for over five years and have received many decorations. In the Reconnaissance Group and the Capturing Group we caught hundreds of officers and soldiers of the Nazi army, and now I am working with you. I was thinking that since I was born in Poland and lived there until the age of 18, I would like to be transferred to the Polish army."

He looked at me and said that I would be making a big mistake, since he could transfer me to the Higher Officers' School to study to become a colonel or even a general. The opportunity was available because of my past success in the Reconnaissance. The Colonel suggested that I should not miss out and, with gratitude, I told him that I would think about it.

Several days later, I went to see him and told him that I had made my decision to be transferred to the Polish army. He was sorry to see me go but he promised to send my resume along with a letter of explanation as to how I came to be with the Russian army and why I wished to transfer to the Polish army now. I was grateful for his help. It would take several weeks for the response.

Two weeks later, Colonel Abramov from the main office came, introduced himself and asked me to sit down. He had received my resume and wanted to talk to me. The transfer I had asked for, transferring from one country's army to another country's army, was the first in history, and he offered me the officers' school. I had great potential in the Russian army since I had a background fighting against the Germans in Reconnaissance in the 385th Division and my division had been named the best in the army, the 385 Krichiowskaia Krasnosamjonaia Oren Suworowa Division. I even had the potential to become a general in the Russian army.

I thanked him for recognizing that I was a good officer, but at that time the country where I was born needed people like me to build up the army and it was my opportunity to do so. Colonel Abramov was very sorry to lose an officer like me, but agreed to send me the transfer papers in several days. He gave me a hug, said he was sorry, and left.

The next day, I went to Ludwigslust to bid farewell to the American officers and to tell them about my transfer to the Polish army. They opened a bottle of Chivas Regal, and we drank until it was time to leave. Then, we hugged and said good-bye.

When I returned to Grabow, I took my assistant to the Transfer Place and introduced him to the staff. I told him to take care of them and said good-bye to everybody. I called the mayor and said goodbye to him also. A few days later, the Colonel called me to his office to tell me he had received my transfer papers. He said that it had been a pleasure working with me, gave me a hug and wished me good luck in the future. He told me that I was an excellent reconnaissance officer and that he would like to have more officers like me, then gave me another hug and handed me the papers.

The next day, I packed my belongings, had breakfast and called the airport for a ticket to Warsaw. There was a flight leaving at 11 a.m., so I left at once and arrived in time to pick up my ticket and board the plane. After a long flight to Warsaw, I disembarked, picked up my suitcase, and checked into a hotel. After a shower, I went to the bar to have a drink and something to eat.

At the bar, I met several people and we started to talk. They wondered how I came to speak Polish and I told them I was born in Poland. They asked me how I became an officer in the Russian army, and I began to tell them my story.

Then, one person said that the Germans did the right thing in the elimination of the Jewish people. I listened as they continued, saying that all the doctors were Jews. I stood up and said that I had known that anti-Semitism was bad in Poland, but I did not think it was quite this bad. They looked at me, thinking that I was a Pole, and I told them that I was a Polish Jew, and I had lost my whole family in the concentration camps and the crematoriums. I told them that I did not fight for and liberate Poland so that they could sit there and have a good time, insulting me and the Jewish people. They were all lucky to be alive, because I eliminated several hundreds of German Nazis.

They all stood up, apologized and left. I asked the bartender for a double vodka with no ice and when I finished my drink, I went to my room to sleep.

The next day, I decided not to enter the Polish army. I called the airport and made a reservation to go to Oświęcim. I boarded a plane for Krakow the following day and after several hours, I arrived in Oświęcim. I checked into a hotel, setting down my suitcase and eating at a restaurant.

The next day, I went back to the concentration camp, Auschwitz. I spent several hours there and brought pictures of some of the Holocaust survivors.

Upon returning to the hotel, I stopped at the bar to have a drink. There were several people there and they were talking about the war and Russia. They all agreed that the Russian army was very strong and then the conversation turned to the Jews. They all said that before the war, their city of Oświęcim was run by Jews. Every store was Jewish, and therefore everything was closed on Saturday. One person said, "I hate the dirty Jews." I listened, and since they were speaking Polish, they thought that I could not understand them.

After I had heard enough, I stood up and said, in Polish, "The Jews are not dirty; they are the same people as anybody else."

I added, "I am Jewish," and told them that I was born right there in Oświęcim, and went to school with one of their friends, who sat next to me in class. They all looked at each other and I called out his name, Jusek Papiersky! He stood up and looked at me and I told him my name was Iser Reifer.

Jusek said, "Yes, I remember you with your side curls." He added, "You were very religious."

"You called us dirty Jews before, and still call us dirty Jews," I said.

"I am an officer in the Russian army! I have been fighting the Germans for over five years and I liberated Poland for you, and you call me a dirty Jew? When you were free you did not fight for yourselves. Russia did the fighting for you, with Jews like myself. We won the war with the elimination of many millions of Nazis. The Russian army lost 20 million brave soldiers and officers. I was in Reconnaissance, and for my bravery I received many decorations. I was also wounded.

"Now I come to our city of Oświęcim where I lived with my family, my mother and father and four brothers, and I have found no one alive! They were sent to the concentration camp, and then to the gas chamber and the crematorium, and you still sit here and call me a dirty Jew.

"I want to tell you something: I asked my colonel to transfer me to the Polish army, because I was born here and the Polish army needs to be built up. But after listening to you and the hatred you have for the Jews, I have to rethink my plans." I got up from my chair, apologized and left the room.

In Oświęcim, I spoke to many Jewish people who had been liberated from the concentration camps, all of whom had lost their families. They said I was lucky to be alive and to have been able to fight the German Nazis. I appreciated what they were saying. Yes I was very fortunate, but it wasn't much comfort since I too had lost my entire family.

All evening, I thought about what I had to do, and fell asleep thinking. After breakfast, I went to the center of the city to meet some people and to start a conversation. They were talking about leaving Poland and considering going to Belgium. I said it was a good idea, and asked them if they knew how to get the appropriate papers. They said that no papers were needed, only the money to pay for the trip. They promised to find out the cost and meet me the next day. When they told me the price, I agreed to go to Belgium. We made an appointment to meet a few days later in the center of town on the sidewalk in front of the police station.

The next day after breakfast, I went to buy a suit, shoes, shirts, socks and undergarments. I returned to the hotel to eat for the last time in my Russian uniform, then went up to my room and changed into my new suit. Suddenly, I looked like a different person. When I went to confirm the date and time to meet with my traveling companions, they at first did not recognize me. I got rid of my uniform and checked out of the hotel, making my way to my companions to begin our journey. It was an unpleasant trip, which I do not want to describe.

Twelve
Leaving Eastern Europe

It was several days before we arrived in Antwerp, Belgium. There, I rented a small furnished apartment on the main street and called my uncle in New York, who was very happy to hear my voice. When I told him I was in Antwerp, he said he would come to see me in a couple of days.

I gave him my address and he asked if I needed any money. I had some money, but I asked him to bring me the address of my uncle Feiner, my mother's brother, who lived in Long Island, New York. My uncle Reifer said that he had spoken to Mr. Feiner after receiving my letter, and they were both proud that I had been in the Russian army fighting the Germans. It was wonderful to be speaking to my uncle Reifer, the youngest of my father's brothers.

I looked around the city and went to a restaurant. I did not speak Flemish, but spoke Yiddish. The owner of the restaurant came to my table and asked me in Yiddish where I came from. I told him Oswiecim and discovered that he was in the concentration camp of Auschwitz. I explained that I had not been in the camp but was born in the city of Oswiecim, fought in the Russian army against Germans, and had just arrived in Antwerp. He asked what I wanted to do here and I answered that I had called my uncle in New York, who would be here in a few days. The owner said that the dinner was on the house, and I thanked him for his kindness and left a tip for the waiter. Before returning to my small apartment, I bought a Flemish newspaper and tried to read it, Since I knew German, it did not seem to be too difficult.

The next morning I went for breakfast at the same restaurant as the evening before, and had 2 scrambled eggs with onions and toast and a cup of coffee.

There was another gentleman sitting at my table and I spoke to him, telling him my name was Alex. He introduced himself as Wolf Boxenbaum, and he showed me the tattoo that the Nazis had put on his arm in the concentration camp. He had lost his parents and now lived in Antwerp with his uncle Kiwu. His uncle and a cousin named Leib Mehlman were all the family he had left.

I told him my full name, Alex Reifer, and that I was born in Oswiecim, where I lived until 1939 when the German army attacked Poland. I told him of how my family had fled when there was a rumor that the Germans were killing 18 year old boys, and how my grandfather blessed me and told me to run away, wishing me to live to be 120 years old. I told him about how I found work in the coal mine and the drugstore before serving in the Russian army in the Reconnaissance department.

We talked for a while about my decorations and how I met the American 82nd division in Ludwigslust. After finishing my story with my arrival in Antwerp, I told Wolf that I was glad to have met him and went back to my room. Once again I called my uncle Reifer, who told me that he would arrive in Antwerp in two days.

The next day, I met again with Wolf Boxenbaum. From that day on, we became friends and still are to this day. I hope to continue our friendship for many more years.

Finally, my uncle Reifer arrived in Antwerp and I met him at the airport. He was happy to see me, and we hugged and got into a taxi to go to a hotel. In the hotel room, he asked me how I was able to survive the past five years, fighting the German army. I told him my life story. He was very pleased to hear all of it, and was very proud to hear about all my decorations and how I handled myself when interrogating the German Nazis that I caught, though also sad that I was wounded.

My uncle asked me what I was planning to do in Antwerp, and I told him that I did not know. Then he said that he had a friend in the diamond business and he would ask him to hire me. I did not know anything about the diamond business, but my uncle assured me that his friend would teach me. After lunch, he called his friend and asked him to meet us at the hotel. Meanwhile, my uncle told me how he had left Vienna for Paris and then traveled with his family through North Africa and Portugal, until arriving in New York City in 1941.

He told me that he had written letters to Oswiecim, but they were all returned to him. He then found out that Jews no longer lived in Oswiecim, as they had all been sent to Sosnowice or Bendin. He began writing letters to Sosnowice and this time, the letters reached their destinations.

My parents and uncles wrote back and told him that they were in bad shape and did not have enough food. They wrote that they were only surviving on water and that the Germans were beating them and calling them very bad names, as were the Polish people, who called them dirty Jews.

My uncle said that he had received several letters from my parents, as well as from his parents and family, until the letters stopped coming. These were the addresses of the family:

My father, Bernard Reifer: Sosnowice, Merkstrasse 7

My uncle, Josef Lauber: Sosnowice, Beskiedenenstrasse 17

My uncle, Issak Hutterer: Sosnowice, Beskiedenstrasse 48/1

My cousin, Israel Iser Lauber: Wadowice, Kirschstrasse 6

As planned, my uncle's friend met us at the hotel, and they were happy to see each other. My uncle introduced me and told him my story of how I had spent 5 years in the Russian army, had only recently arrived, and was interested in starting a new life.

The man offered to teach me how to sell diamonds. He spoke to me in Yiddish, but told me that I would have to learn Flemish very quickly. Since I already spoke German, I figured it would be easy.

He gave me his business card and told me to come

to his office in the Diamond Bourse on Monday morning. He would register me in the Diamond Ring and begin showing me the parcels of diamonds.

Diamonds are sold by the carat. There are 100 points per carat. 50 points is ½ carat, 25 points is ¼ carat, and so forth. First, I was shown one point diamonds, and then larger ones. After my first lesson, my uncle's friend asked me to come back in a couple of days, when he would explain the best technique for selling them, adding that he hoped I would be successful.

My uncle was very pleased and invited me for lunch. He offered to contact my uncle Feiner, whose address I gave him, and ask his help in preparing the papers for my immigration to the United States.

When I returned to the office to learn more about the diamonds I would be selling, my uncle's friend invited me to take a seat and opened the safe, bringing out diamond parcels, a pair of tweezers and a loupe (magnifying glass). He picked up a one point diamond with the tweezer and began to show me how to judge the quality. If there were any black spots, he explained, the diamond was of lesser quality and therefore of lower price, and without them, the quality was better and the price higher. I stayed in his office practicing for many hours.

When I returned the next day, I had a registration card for the Diamond Ring prepared for me. One of the assistants showed me how to sell diamonds and what I should be charging. A few hours later, we went to the Diamond Ring and sat down at a table.

Some people came up to me and asked what kind

of diamonds I had for sale. I explained that they were quality melees (one to five points) for $300 per carat. After checking the goods, they offered $250 per carat. These diamonds were of good quality, and I knew that they were worth more. I refused to sell them for less, so they rechecked and offered $275 per carat for five carat diamonds. I agreed, and told them that they had to pay in cash, either American dollars or Belgian francs. I told them I would return with the five carats in an hour.

I returned to the office of my uncle's friend, who was pleased with the price, and gave me a five carat parcel which I brought to the customer. He checked the parcel and paid me, completing my first deal. I brought the money to my uncle's friend, who gave me 10% commission of $137.50, the first money I made in Antwerp. I called my uncle Reifer and happily reported that I had been successful in making a sale.

A few days later my uncle departed for New York. I accompanied him to the airport and thanked him for coming to visit me and for helping me find work. I kissed him and expressed the hope that we would both be together again soon in America. He promised to work with my uncle Feiner to arrange my emigration to America.

When I returned to my apartment, I wrote my uncle Feiner a letter, telling him that I was in Antwerp and all about my uncle Reifer. I didn't give him too much detail, just that my uncle Reifer would fill him in on what I had been doing from 1939 until 1946.

The next morning at work, I was given more parcels of diamonds, which I sold. I was slowly beginning to learn the diamond business. I learned the difference between a full cut diamond and a single cut, the quality of a VS, a VS1 and VVS diamond: the good, very good, and excellent.

Almost every day, I met my friend Wolf Boxenbaum for dinner. Often, the conversations turned to his time in the concentration camp. He showed me the number tattooed on his forearm. I shared a little about my past as well. Sometimes after dinner we would go to a movie or watch wrestling or boxing matches.

Soon other friends joined in, people like Gogush. There were others whose names I do not remember. We would go to the waterfront, called Santanica, or to the city of Knocke for the weekend. During the week, we frequented the Cafe Blum on Festing Straat, or else the dairy restaurant called Preiger.

After a few months, the diamond business slowed down and I was not able to make any money. I needed to look elsewhere. In the Diamond Ring there was a restaurant where I had coffee and toast in the morning. The owner, Mr. Oscar Felsenstein, often spoke with me while I ate. When I told him that I was not making any money, he asked me what other skills I had. I said that when I was younger, I used to carve items from wood and food.

He took me into the kitchen, which was in the basement, and asked me to show him. I told him that I would need a pen, a knife and a raw potato or turnip. In about five minutes, I had carved a rose from a potato. I suggested that I could make them yellow or red, with food coloring.

This he really liked, and offered me a job at parties,

Bar Mitzvahs and weddings. I let him know that I could also carve fruit. He had a party the coming weekend, and asked me to begin work then.

I arrived at his kitchen on at 8 a.m. on Friday and was introduced to the chef, Anton, who gave me a white jacket, an apron and a white hat. Chef Anton asked me what I needed, and I told him to give me a few potatoes, a pen and a knife and I began carving roses. The chef liked the roses, and asked for more.

He brought me a watermelon, a cantaloupe, a honeydew melon, cucumbers, oranges, grapefruit and radishes. From the watermelon I carved a wishing well, baskets from the melons and small flowers from the radishes. The next day I decorated the large table. Both Anton and Mr. Felsenstein were very pleased. The party was a sensation, and Mr. Felsenstein received many new bookings.

On Monday, I went to see my uncle's friend to let him know that I would no longer be selling diamonds. I thanked him for the opportunity, and then I left to pursue my newfound career.

Not long after that, I was invited to an exclusive restaurant, called Atlass. The owner, Mr. Atlass, came to our table and introduced himself. He had admired my carvings at several parties and asked if I was interested in doing some parties for him.

I was anxious for the additional work, but I worried about what Oscar Felsenstein might think. However, to my surprise, Mr. Atlass told me that Felsenstein already knew that Atlass wanted to hire me. With that settled, he paid for my dinner, and I was on my way.

With my new schedule, I was busy most weekends. One day, Mr. Felsenstein approached me when I was working and asked if I could help him out during the week as headwaiter in his restaurant. The following Monday I started at the position, Now I was busy the entire week. I liked my new job and got along quite well with all of the other waiters.

Almost every week, I would receive letters from both my uncles saying that soon I should receive the papers required to come to the United States. My uncle Feiner and I hadn't met yet, and he was anxious to get to know me. My uncle Reifer wrote that my cousin Ecia, who was married to Rabbi Naftali Eckstein, was now in New York.

Ecia had been the cousin I was closest to when we were children. I used to help her in her father's leatherware store, which was in the center of the city, next to the police station. My uncle would pay me 5 Groschen, the equivalent to 1 cent American. When I was 13 years old and Bar Mitzvahed, Ecia embroidered the bag for my tefillin with needlepoint. She had made much needlepoint for my grandparents and parents when she was a young girl, including pictures. I was eager to see her again in New York.

In Antwerp, life was simple: after work as head waiter, I would meet my friend Wolf Boxenbaum and go to the movies, boxing or wrestling matches, or to dance at The Follies, a disco. Some weekends, when I did not have to do a party, we went to Knocke, a resort on the beach, or to Blankenberg or Spa, where we would often play Rummy and bridge, or soccer.

In the Diamond Ring, where I had worked previously, there was a gentleman selling 14 carat gold jewelry. He approached me and asked if I wanted a diamond ring made for me, and showed me some styles. I picked a design with a 0.44 carat diamond set in 14 carat gold. He quoted the price and I agreed. A couple of days later he brought me the ring, engraved with my initials, IR, which I am wearing to this day.

Around this time, my uncle Reifer sent me some letters he had received from my parents and grandparents. They had been sent from Sosnowice, to where they had been deported from Oswiecim. They wrote that they were not able to bring anything with them, and although in Oswiecim they had a nice business and their children all went to school, now they had nothing, were very poor and had no food or winter clothing. It was unbelievable that my parents and my brothers had been so hungry. How could something like this happen?

Here is the translation of one letter from 1941:

My dear son Ernest Iser,

I must tell you that the Germans threw us out from our house in Oswiecim and sent us to Sosnowice. They did not let us take anything with us. The situation is very bad and we do not know what will happen. The Germans hate us, and call us very bad names and the rumor is that they will send the entire Jewish population to the concentration camps. Please write often. Meanwhile, I am still alive or you can say existing, with our dear mother, my dear wife.

Best regards,

Your father Mayer Reifer.

There were a number of letters written in Yiddish by my father to my uncle Reifer in 1940 and 1941. After they had arrived in Sosnowice, they looked for a place to live and found a room on Markt Strasse No.7. There was not even any furniture. My father implored his brother to send some clothes and some food, because they had nothing to eat. He wrote that the situation was desperate, although they were still fairly healthy. My father also asked for some old shoes for his children, because they had none for the winter. He hoped to soon receive a letter from my uncle soon and finished the letter with regards from his wife and children, and signed it: your brother Bernard Reifer, Sosnowice Markt Strasse No 7, Deutschland.

There was also a letter written by my uncle Isaac Hutterer, who had married my aunt Rosa, my father's sister. After they were married, they had moved to Berlin, where Isaac studied law and became an attorney. In 1933, Hitler came to power, and soon thereafter the Hutterers and their two children left Berlin and returned to Oswiecim. They moved into one of Isaac's father's apartments, opened a bicycle shop and did well. The letter was dated January 15, 1941, from Rosa and Isaac Hutterer, Pilsudskistrasse 7, Sosnowice, Poland.

My dear Ernest and Friedl,

We have received your letter from Lisbon, before you arrived in America, and were happy to hear from you, since we had not heard from you for a year. The letter you wrote on December 27, 1940 to our parents has also arrived. I am letting you know that our dear grandfather did not feel well on Sunday, January 12, 1941 at 4:30pm and even though he tried to comfort himself on the sofa, he passed away. He left this world for the holy world. For us, that day was truly unbelievable, everybody was crying. The whole family came together to prepare for the funeral and there were several hundred people to walk behind the casket.

My grandfather was the finest person in my life. I was his eyes, after his cataract operation failed and he lost his sight. He had been a prominent religious scholar in Oswiecim. I do not know old he was, but in my life he will always be remembered as the finest, nicest person. I am very sorry that I wasn't able to attend his funeral.

Thirteen
Journey to America

In the fall of 1952, I received the immigration papers from my dear uncles Reifer and Feiner to come to the United States of America. Along with the papers was a boat ticket for me to travel on the SS *Harvester America*. The ship was to sail from France, so I received a Titre de Voyage, a Reisebeweis, a type of passport, to go from Belgium to France. It showed my name, Iser Reifer, my address in Antwerp, Feistingstraat.42, and was dated January 15, 1952.

Soon, I traveled to France and on November 11, 1952 at 3 p.m. , I boarded the ship *Harvester*. I went to my cabin and began writing a letter in Yiddish, translated into English, to my friend Mayson Betty at Lamonir Str. 33, Antwerp, Belgium. It was returned to my uncle's address. It said:

Dear family and friends,

Today is my happy day. I am on the ship *Harvester* bound for the United States to be united with my uncle Reifer and his family. The ship began moving from this port of Bologne, France, and I was standing on deck. There was a heavy wind, so I returned to my cabin and took a pill to prevent seasickness and felt fine. At 5 p.m. , I had tomato soup, a veal cutlet and a cup of coffee and am now writing this letter, which you will read when I will already be in the United States. The ship *Harvester* weights 2000 tons and one feels the movement only a little because it has a cargo of only 1800 tons. I noticed one passenger not feeling well, but on the other side, some were playing cards. The motors of the ship are very noisy.

I spoke to many passengers. Some were from Hungary, having recently lived in Belgium, and several were from Tarnopol, Poland; some were from Paris and three passengers, the Mendelsons, were from Warsaw. They had left Poland in 1939 for Russia, and in 1946 came to Paris. I politely declined to join those playing cards, since I had no interest in this activity. Instead, I had a snack and retired to my cabin at 9 p.m.

The next morning, November 12, 1952, at 6:30a.m., I woke up, ate breakfast and went out on deck to look at the Atlantic Ocean. The ocean was quiet and still the ship was moving at 60 miles per hour. I hoped that the rest of the trip would be this excellent. The sun was nice with a little breeze, fantastic!

I spent two hours on deck, then had lunch in the dining room: vegetable soup, meat with rice, a glass of milk and some coffee. I was surprised to see that milk was always on the table, just like wine in France. I felt good.

Back on deck until 2 p.m. , then back to my cabin to

rest, not because I was tired, but because there was nothing else to do. I decided to start studying English, using a dictionary. I began pronouncing sentences and picked it up quickly. I seemed to be very good.

At 3:30 p.m., somebody knocked on my cabin door and said that I needed to be on deck in 10 minutes for a drill. I was told that there would be an alarm, and then all passengers were to come with their life jackets. The alarm sounded and everybody gathered by the rafting boats that had the same numbers as their cabins. Mine was number 2. After the alarm stopped sounding and the drill was complete, I returned to my cabin, removed the life jacket and went to the dining room to have a bite to eat.

The following day, the ship was shaking, but I had slept quite well that night, so it did not affect me. I took a shower, had breakfast, went out on deck and lay down on a lounging chair. The sun was very hot and I stayed out for a long time, until it was time for me to go back to my cabin to continue my study of English.

After dinner, I washed some of my laundry. The ship moved so slowly, it reminded me of the way a religious Jew moves very slowly when he prays, like I used to do when I was young. The weather was nice, but the ship was shaking, which did not bother me, as long as I stayed outside for an hour before going to sleep.

The night was quiet, but the next day, November 14th, there were strong winds, so I returned to my cabin after breakfast. Many passengers were seasick and did not feel well, but I was okay. Same schedule: study English, eat lunch and dinner. Again I was invited to join some passengers for bridge, and I accepted until it was time to go to sleep.

It was very windy outside and I could feel the ship moving. The table, chairs, and my two suitcases slid around the cabin as the ship rocked, and I feared the ship would tip over. It stormed until 1a.m., when the wind calmed down, so I could go on deck and lay down. I felt like singing all the songs I knew before returning to the cabin.

The next day the winds had subsided and the ship was moving at 24 miles per hour. The day passed, playing cards and talking with Mr. Mendelson. We exchanged jokes until 10PM .

The next day, the weather was quiet and the ship moved slowly. I realized that during the entire trip, I had never seen another vessel on the ocean. I was happy to know that in a few days we would arrive in Norfolk, Virginia. Meanwhile, another strong storm came up, so that the ship again shook to the point that I feared it would sink.

Finally, after a 10-day voyage, the ship docked in Norfolk, Virginia on November 21, 1952. The next day, I called my uncle Reifer in New York to advise him when I would arrive by American Airlines. I was so happy to see him when he picked me up from the airport and I embraced and kissed him.

He took me to his home, at 410 Central Park West in New York, and invited me for dinner, together with my aunt Friedl and their children Mary and Hans. We had a very nice time together. They asked me about the war and I told them about my five years in the Russian army.

The next day, my uncle took me to meet my uncle Feiner, my mother's oldest brother. We traveled to Rhode Island, where my uncle Feiner had his factory. This was the first time I met him. When we embraced, he said he was very happy to see me. He introduced me to his two sons, Sol and Philip, who were working with him in the factory, and then showed me this big place and the manufacturing of ash cans.

My uncle Reifer left and my uncle Feiner took me to his home and introduced me his wife, who had prepared dinner. They asked me how I came to Russia and about the army there, then invited me to their living room to

Alex Reifer, 1970

watch television. They showed me the room where I could rest for the night.

The next morning, after I ate breakfast and thanked my uncle's family for their hospitality, I left to visit my cousin Ecia and her husband, Rabbi Naftali Eckstein, who had a fish market in Manhattan. They were married in 1937 and in 1938, she gave birth to a son, Morris. They were financially secure and had a maid to take care of the baby. In 1939, when the war broke out, they left Morris in care of the maid and fled the city. The Germans caught them and they were taken to the concentration camp, separated from each other.

After the war, Ecia was liberated and found the maid with whom she had left her child, an effort which took a number of days. When Ecia walked into the maid's house to retrieve her son, the maid was stunned. When Ecia kissed Morris, both began to cry--Ecia because she had missed him so much and Morris because he was scared of her, since he did not remember her. He ran from his mother to the maid, whom he considered his mother. Ecia told the maid that she wanted her son back and that she would pay her for taking care of him these past years.

So finally she took Morris, who was crying and screaming, and travelled with him to Germany. She was reunited with her husband through the efforts of a Jewish organization. They were unbelievably happy to have found each other and their son. Slowly, Morris got reacquainted with his parents and began to speak Yiddish after several weeks. Soon thereafter they left for the United States and opened their fish market.

When I visited them there, they were very happy to see me, as was I to see them alive. They invited me to their apartment to meet Morris, who was a very nice boy, and over dinner they told me about the problems they had in the concentration camps and how Ecia found her son.

Having been welcomed by both my uncles and reunited with my cousin Ecia, I was now ready to settle in what would become my Promised Land.